BASQUE SOCIOLINGUI

C000063160

Estibaliz Amorrortu r(
in Basque Philology f
Bilbao, in 1992; her M.A. in English from the Uni.
of Nevada, Reno; and her M.A. and Ph.D. in Linguistics
from the University of Southern California in 2000. She
has taught Basque language at the University of Nevada,
Reno; Language, Society and Culture, as a teaching
assistant, at the University of Southern California; and
the History of English at the University of the Basque
Country in Vitoria-Gasteiz. She is a professor in the
Department of Basque Philology at the University of
Deusto, Bilbao, since 2001.

Her primary research interests include Basque sociolinguistics, language contact, and discourse analysis.

Estibaliz Amorrortu

Basque Sociolinguistics
Language, Society, and Culture

Basque Textbooks Series

Center for Basque Studies
University of Nevada, Reno

This book was published with generous financial
support from the Basque Government.

Library of Congress Cataloging-in-Publication Data

Amorrortu, Estibaliz, 1969–
    Basque Sociolinguistics : language, society, and
culture / Estibaliz Amorrortu.
        p. cm.—(Basque textbooks series)
    Includes bibliographical references and index.
    ISBN 978-1-877802-22-5 (paperback)
    ISBN 978-1-877802-23-2 (hardcover)
    ISBN 978-1-877802-24-9 (compact disk)
    1. Basque language—Social aspects. 2. Sociolinguis-
tics—Spain—País Vasco. 3. Basque language—History.
4. Languages in contact. I.Title. II. Series.
    PH5024.75.A46 2003
    306.44'0946'6--dc22

                                    2003023231

Published by the Center for Basque Studies
University of Nevada, Reno /322
Reno, Nevada 89557-0012.

Printed in the United States of America

CONTENTS

Preface

THE BASQUE language plays a central role in Basque
society and culture. Basques call themselves
euskaldunak 'speakers of Basque', and the language is
one of the most important elements defining their identity. The main objective of *Basque Sociolinguistics: Language, Society, and Culture* is to provide a comprehen-
sive overview of the social and cultural aspects of the
Basque language, highlighting the role of language in
Basque politics and cultural and social practices, as well
as the influence of social forces on the language.

Basque Sociolinguistics is directed to the beginner; the
topics are introduced assuming little knowledge of
either sociolinguistics or Basque issues. Readers interested in exploring topics with greater depth should con-
sult the resources listed at the end of each chapter. In
addition to sections entitled Required Readings and Suggested Readings, most chapters include the heading
Internet Resources. A great deal of information about
the topics covered in this book can be found on the
World Wide Web; unfortunately, some of the websites
are not available in English ("Basque only" or "Spanish
and Basque only" is noted where applicable).

Many chapters have an Important Concepts section in
order to guide readers to the most significant issues. In
addition, words which are printed in **bold italics** on
their first occurrence are defined in the Glossary at the
back of the book, which is followed by a List of Abbreviations. The lesson section at the end of each chapter also
includes a heading for learning objectives and ends with
questions for further thinking about the topics covered.

The book is divided into four parts. Part One includes
introductory chapters on Basque history, failed efforts to

link Basque genetically to other languages, and a brief description of the structure of Basque. Part Two assesses the social and geographical regression of Basque through history, and introduces readers to the current sociolinguistic situation in the Basque Country, addressing quantitative data relative to the number of speakers, situations of use, and attitudes toward Basque and government intervention to reverse its minority status, and pointing to some important issues for the present and future of Basque. Part Three covers language variation from the point of view of linguistics. Basque is examined from two perspectives: its internal variation, with a focus on regional, social, and situational variation; and the change produced by the external influence of other languages. Finally, Part Four explores the relationship of language, identity, and culture, and covers topics such as nationalism and ethnicity displays as they relate to the Basque language, ethnolinguistic vitality, and gender variation.

Acknowledgments

I STARTED working on this book in 2000, after Joseba
Zulaika, Director of the Center of Basque Studies at
the University of Nevada, Reno, asked me to teach an
online course on Basque sociolinguistics. During my
work on the manuscript from October 2000 to February
2003, I received generous financial support from the
Department of Education, Universities, and Research of
the Basque Government through a postdoctoral research
grant. I am also grateful to Roland Vázquez for editing
the class materials and to Nere Amenabar for preparing
the Internet version.

Joseba later asked me to work the class notes and
materials into a textbook to be published in a series of
books on Basque topics.

I owe a special word of gratitude to the professors who
helped introduce me to sociolinguistics, and especially
to Ed Finegan and Carmen Silva-Corvalán. Our long discussions during my doctoral program at the University
of Southern California contributed greatly to my formation as a sociolinguist and to my realizing the importance of social issues in linguistics.

Last but not least, I would like to express my gratitude
to all the staff of the Center of Basque Studies at the University of Nevada, Reno for their support and assistance
through the years, and especially to Joseba Zulaika.

1 · The Basque people
Historical Introduction

IN THIS chapter, we will briefly review the history of the Basques. Basque history has profoundly affected the development of the language, culture, and society. The history of the Basque people demonstrates their unique culture and social organization as well as the influence of surrounding peoples. Although many European languages and cultures have disappeared, the Basque language and culture have remained distinctive; they have managed to survive the passing centuries while others have faded away.

Basque social and institutional organization have had to adjust to externally imposed conditions. The unique Basque system of customary law, based on generally egalitarian and democratic principles and orally transmitted custom, gave rise to the foral system, a kind of self-government manifested in the political, economic, and judicial realms. Bilateral agreements based on the foral system determined the relationships between the Basques and their neighbors for centuries. The growing power of the Spanish and French states, however, brought about the decline of many features intrinsic to the Basque social and political system.

Although the Basque culture and language have remained distinct over time, Basque speakers have been exposed to contact with a variety of cultures and speakers of other languages. During prehistoric times, the Celts lived among them. Later, Basque speakers were influenced by the Romans and the introduction of christianization, a fact ascertainable from the high number of old **borrowings** from Latin into Basque. See S. Segura and J. M. Etxebarria (1996), for a thorough description

Table 1-1
Borrowings from Latin into Basque

Latin	Basque	English
hortus	ortua	garden
caelum	zerua	ceiling
angelus	aingerua	angel
baculum	makila, makulua	stick

of the Latin influence on the Basque language. Table 1-1 shows four examples.

Peoples of other cultures have, of course, influenced the Basques for centuries, especially the Spaniards and the French and, in recent decades, the Americans.

The language is often said to be the main element unifying the Basque people, though its importance as a symbol of Basque identity has varied depending on the historical period. The Basque language, Euskara, itself associates Basqueness with speaking Basque (*euskalduna* means both 'Basque' and 'one who speaks the Basque language'). The first writers in the Basque language stressed its function in linking the Basque people. With the late nineteenth-century rise of nationalism, language took on a key role in the construction of the Basque nation. Today, Basques differ in the importance they give to Euskara, and the Basque language often lies at the heart of the debate between Basque and Spanish nationalists.

CURRENTLY, the culturally and ethnically Basque territories are divided into three political entities. The Basque Government is the government of the Basque Autonomous Community (BAC), the home of most Basques and the site of the majority of government efforts to promote Basque culture and language. The

Basque-speaking areas
The Basque language was once spoken in a much larger area. This map shows the Basque-speaking areas in the middle of the 20th century in lighter gray. Contact areas, regions where local Basque is still used although there is significant language loss, appear in darker gray. Light areas represent monolingual Spanish regions.
Map adapted from Intxausti (1990:29).

Foral Community of Navarre is another **autonomous community** within Spain. And, finally, the French Basque Country is trying to become a political and administrative entity separate from the Département des Pyrenées Atlantiques to which it currently belongs. Although unified by language and culture, these three political entities vary in their level of self-government, and assign differing degrees of importance to the Basque language and culture.

HISTORICAL SKETCH: MAIN POINTS OF INTEREST

1. Prehistory: The Basque Country has been inhabited by the same people since Paleolithic times.
2. Linguistic and genetic evidence shows the uniqueness of the Basques with respect to other European peoples.
3. Romanization: There is strong Romanization in the south, but contact almost everywhere. Strabo and Ptolemy's reports on Basque people.
4. The Visigoths were unable to conquer the Basque Country.
5. Iñigo de Arista founded the Kingdom of Pamplona around 824; Sancho Garces III, the Great, was the king of Navarre from 1000 to 1035. At this time, all Basque territories were unified as a single political entity for the only time in history. Although the Kingdom of Navarre was Basque-speaking, the lingua navarrorum (Basque) never served higher functions. Latin, Occitan (Langue D'Oc), and Navarrese Romance were the written languages.
6. Middle Ages: Urbanization. Beginning of the rural/urban dichotomy.
7. Twelfth century: Whaling became significant beginning in the twelfth century. Beginning of development of incipient Basque-based pidgin varieties.

8. Early thirteenth century: Distinct political bands were constituted: "War of the Bands." Clan wars between Oñacinos and Gamboinos until 1474.

9. Fifteenth century: Basque hegemony in Spanish trade with Western Europe. Basques were also very involved in the first voyages to the new territories, and Basque fishermen reached Iceland by 1412. Elkano, who completed the first trip around the world, was Basque.

10. Sixteenth century: Basque fishermen reached North America by the sixteenth century.

11. Heavy Basque migration to America: The system of fueros both facilitated and forced the emigration of many Basques. The inheritance system did not allow for division of the household among the siblings. Therefore, a single sibling inherited the entire household. This rule forced the others to migrate or turn to religious life. The principle of "hidalguía universal" granted every Basque noble status, which also facilitated their passage to the Americas. Lastly, as a consequence of the foral agreements with Castile, Basques had trade freedom and became very influential during the colonization of America.

12. Seventeenth century: Decline of the Spanish Empire. Relations between the Basques and the Spanish state were still good.

13. Eighteenth century: Centralist Bourbon monarchy in Spain. Strain began to develop in relations between the Basques and the Spanish monarchy. Following the French Revolution in 1789, the northern Basque provinces were abolished, and use of the Basque language was prohibited. Imposition by Napoleon of the new French legal system, based on Roman law. Harsh attack against Basque language,

culture, and social organization in the North.
French centralization remains into the present.

14. Nineteenth century: The First Spanish liberal constitution in 1812. The new Spanish liberal government
attacked the Basque foral system, but encouraged
industry and commerce, which benefited the Basque
bourgeoisie. The first Carlist War in 1833 divided
the Basque people into two camps: defenders of the
old system (allied with King Carlos) and liberals
(allied with Carlos's nephew, Isabel). The victory of
the latter in subsequent wars brought increasing
restriction of the Basque foral system. After the second Carlist War in 1873, the "Conciertos Económi-
cos" stood as the last vestiges of the foral system.
The end of the nineteenth century saw the rise of
Basque nationalism with Sabino Arana. Little by little, the language would occupy a central role in
political ideology.

15. 1923–1930: Primo de Rivera established a right-wing
dictatorship in Spain.

16. 1931–1936: Second Spanish Republic. Rise in public
displays of Basque identity.

17. 1936: A right-wing military coup against the Republic government provoked a civil war and forty years
of dictatorship. Very harsh repression. Mass migration to the United States and Latin America. Basque
language and cultural expression were banned. In
the 1960s, a widespread grassroots movement in
favor of Basque language and culture developed.

18. 1970s: Transition to democracy in Spain.

19. 1980s: Beginning of government language planning
in favor of Basque.

Lesson one

LEARNING OBJECTIVES

1. Understand that a unique language, culture, and form of social organization have survived through history, although they were influenced by the ways of surrounding peoples.
2. Assess the role of language as a symbol of Basque identity.
3. Become acquainted with political and administrative divisions in the Basque historic territories, and start appreciating the influence of political and administrative aspects on the sociolinguistic development of the Basque language.
4. Learn the main historical facts that characterize the Basque community and briefly explain the current sociolinguistic situation of Basque.

REQUIRED READING

Trask, R. L. 1997. *The History of Basque*, 1–35. London and New York: Routledge.

Trask, R. L. (n.d.b) "FAQs about Basque and the Basques," 1–6: http://www.cogs.susx.ac.uk/users/larryt/basque.faqs.html

SUGGESTED READING

Kurlansky, M. 1999. *The Basque History of the World*, 18–42. London: Jonathan Cape.

Trask, R. L. (n.d.c) "Some Important Basque Words (And a Bit of Culture)," 1–17: http://www.cogs.susx.ac.uk/users/larryt/basque.words.html

---

INTERNET RESOURCES

Note: As mentioned in the Preface, the Internet provides a good deal of valuable information for readers of this book. At the end of most chapters, Internet addresses related to the topics covered are provided. Unless otherwise indicated, all sites have an English version. However, English versions often provide less information than the Basque or Spanish versions. Since Internet addresses often change, readers should become acquainted with Basque search engines (aurki, kaixo, jalgi), which can be used to update or find information. The following sites provide links to pages that cover topics related to many of the issues discussed in this book:

http://www.aurki.com (only available in Basque)
http://www.kaixo.com (only available in Basque and
    Spanish)
http://www.jalgi.com
Blas Uberuaga's Basque webpage offers a huge amount
    of information on Basque topics and many links to
    other important pages:
    http://www.buber.net/Basque/

WRITTEN LESSON FOR SUBMISSION
1. Describe the traits that have defined Basque people
   through history. Include social, political, and linguistic elements in your answer.
2. Explain the Basque foral system and compare it to
   other government systems with which you are familiar. Do you think the foral system influenced the
   maintenance of Basque cultural and linguistic distinctiveness? How so?

2 · The Basque language
External history

BASQUE HAS been in contact with other languages to varying degrees depending on the period and the region. The Romans mentioned a variety of tribes living in the southern region of the Pyrenees: the Vascones, the Varduli, the Verones, the Caristii, and the Autrigones. Although there is no direct evidence that these tribes were Basque-speaking, the territories they occupied coincide with today's Basque dialectal boundaries. Before the onset of Romanization, both Basque and an Indo-European language were probably spoken in certain parts of the Basque-speaking territory.

Shortly after the fourth century, Basque speakers moved to Rioja and Burgos. Coromines's toponymy work indicates that Basque was once spoken on both sides of the Pyrenees, as far east as the now-Catalan-speaking valley of Aran. Use of Basque, along with that of Hebrew and Arabic, was prohibited in the fourteenth-century Huescan market. The prohibition of these non-Romance languages provides evidence of the multilingual nature of the region at the time.

With regard to written forms of Euskara, the first materials written in a language close to Basque were the Aquitanian inscriptions, representing an ancestral form of Basque. The pagan divinities' names shown on the inscriptions are fairly transparent in modern Basque. Nevertheless, the early medieval Emilian Glosses are considered the first testimonies of the Basque language: A bilingual student glossed a Latin text in Romance and in Basque. Multilingualism among the more educated was not unusual in medieval times.

Other important old texts are the Reja de San Millán document (1025), which shows that aspiration [h] was

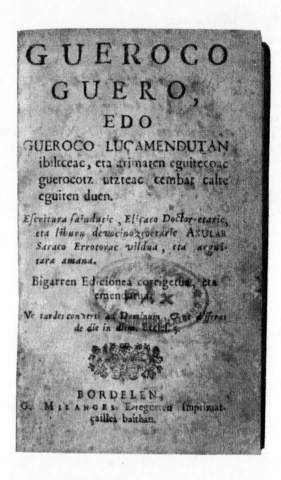

Literary Dialects

Religious writer Axular already pointed to regional differences when he published in 1643 *Gueroco guero*, shown in this photograph. The school of Sare, and its leader Axular, contributed greatly to the creation of Labourdin literary dialect.

still present in Araban Basque; Picaud's list of vocabulary; and testimonies of Basque pidgins used among locals and Basque fishermen along the Canadian and Icelandic coasts. We will take a closer look at Basque-based pidgins in Chapter 16.

In 1545, the first book was published in Basque: Etxepare's *Linguae Vasconum Primitiae*. By the time Etxepare, Leizarraga, and Ohienart wrote the early books in Basque, dialectal differences were quite marked, and definitely larger than during the tenth and eleventh centuries. Already showing modern dialectal variation, four **literary dialects** developed: Labourdin, Gipuzkoan, Bizkaian, and Souletin. The historical promotion of four different **varieties** for standard (mainly literary and religious) use made the spread of Batua, the unified variety of Basque, more difficult at the end of the twentieth century.

Another important characteristic of the external history of Basque is its minority status. Even when most Basques were monolingual, the Basque language did not serve high functions; it was not used for educational and administrative purposes until the end of the twentieth century. All official documents were traditionally written in Latin or the Romance languages. The Basque elite often shifted to using Spanish, and Basque was considered unsuitable for high cultural functions until the eighteenth century, when apologists such a Larramendi defended its purity and capacity to express complex ideas.

THE MINORITY status of Basque has not only been situational. Basque has suffered increasing social and geographical recession. On one hand, influential social groups, such as the nobility, bourgeoisie, and church, often shifted to using Romance languages. On the other, Basque has lost geographical space to

IZIOQUI DUGU GUEC AJUTUEZDUGU

Emilian Glosses
Glosses are comments written next to a text in order to aid the reader understand it. This illustration shows the early medieval Emilian glosses, the first testimonies of the Basque language. Although we can recognize the gloss as being clearly Basque, we cannot fully understand it even with the help of the original Latin text.

Romance languages from the boundaries toward the Pyrenees, as well as in urban centers, especially during the past century.

MORE recently, with the underground popular movement in favor of teaching the Basque language which started at the end of the Franco dictatorship, a new era has begun for Basque. With the transition to democracy, most language planning has become the responsibility of government institutions. Recent decades have witnessed a great expansion of Basque language and culture, owing in part to an active policy of promotion and planning. The Basque language is now taught and used in publication and almost all other situations. In addition, a new variety has been developed for standard and official use.

Main Points of Interest in the External History of Basque

1. Pre-Roman times: Aquitanian form of Basque, Proto-Basque. The forms found in the Aquitanian inscriptions are directly related to Modern Basque: Nescato (Modern Basque neskato 'girl'), Cison (Modern Basque gizon 'man'), Andere (Modern Basque andere 'woman'), Sembe (Modern Basque seme 'son').
2. After the fourth century: Basques and their language expand to Rioja and Burgos.
3. Tenth century: Emilian Glosses, first words written in Basque. Although the glosses are clearly Basque, we cannot understand their meaning.
4. Twelfth century: Picaud collected a list of Basque words: ardum 'wine' (Modern Basque ardo), araign (Modern Basque arrain), elicera 'to the church' (Modern Basque elizara), gari 'wheat' (Modern Basque gari), for instance.
5. 1545: Etxepare published the first book entirely in Basque: Linguae Vasconum Primitiae.
6. 1571: Leizarraga's translation of the Bible.
7. Seventeenth century: High social status of the language in the north—the school of Sare (around Axular) and Ohienart. Development of literary dialects (Labourdin and Souletin, respectively).
8. Seventeenth and eighteenth centuries: Geographical recession in Navarre and Araba.
9. Eighteenth century: Larramendi wrote a grammar and dictionary based on Gipuzkoan, and apologetic works in favor of Basque.

10. Mid-nineteenth century: Prince Bonaparte's dialectal classification. Bonaparte not only laid the groundwork for Basque regional dialectology, but he raised the social prestige of Basque internationally.

11. Nineteenth century: Mogel became one of the most important proponents of the Bizkaian literary dialect.

12. Nineteenth and twentieth centuries: Large-scale immigration of Spanish speakers to the Basque Country due to industrialization (1876–1914). Rise of nationalism in the nineteenth century: the language became a symbol of Basque nationality, which provoked puristic attitudes toward the language.

13. 1918: First Congress of Basque Studies: the Academy was founded with the objective of codifying orthography, modernizing lexicon, and standardizing the language. Codification of Batua (the unified variety of Basque), starting in 1968.

14. 1960s: Important popular urban movement in favor of Basque—the creation of ikastolas and gaueskolas.

15. 1980s: Beginning of conscious policy and planning in support of the Basque language.

Lesson two

LEARNING OBJECTIVES

Note: The reader need not memorize all the historical details (exact dates, for instance) mentioned in this chapter. The main objective is to situate the Basque language in its sociohistorical context. Many issues raised in this chapter will be explored in more depth in subsequent chapters.

1. Understand the social and geographical regression of Basque through history.
2. Examine the historical minority status of Basque: restricted use of Basque for high functions even at times when most of the population was Basque monolingual.
3. Note the different degrees of bilingualism across time, areas, and social groups.

REQUIRED READING

Trask, R. L. 1997. "An External History of the Language," in *The History of Basque*, 35–49. London and New York: Routledge.

Zuazo, K. 1995. "The Basque Country and the Basque Language: An Overview of the External History of the Basque Language," in J. I. Hualde, J. A. Lakarra, and R. L. Trask (eds.), *Towards a History of the Basque Language*, 5–30. Amsterdam/Philadelphia: John Benjamins Publ.

SUGGESTED READING

Intxausti, J. 1995. *Euskal Herria the Country of the Basque Language*. Vitoria-Gasteiz: Basque Government Press.

Tejerina, B. 1992. "Los Procesos Histórico y Social del Euskara," in *Nacionalismo y Lengua*, 73–111. Madrid: Siglo XXI.

INTERNET RESOURCES

Estornés Lasa's Basque Encyclopedia is online thanks to Eusko Ikaskuntza. This multivolume work was published in Spanish. Basque Encyclopedia: http://www.euskomedia.org:8080/euskomedia_e/index.jsp

Eusko Ikaskuntza homepage:
http://www.eusko-ikaskuntza.org/en/home/

WRITTEN LESSON FOR SUBMISSION
1. Why do you think four literary dialects developed in Basque rather than a single strong one?
2. Would you expect transfer from other languages into Basque from what you know so far about the history of Basque people?

3 · The origins of Basque

LANGUAGES are always in the process of changing. Only dead languages, such as Latin, do not. As a result of linguistic change, a single language may split into several languages over time, just as Vulgar Latin became Spanish, French, and Italian. Most European languages are, in fact, the heirs of a language family called Indo-European. For instance, the Germanic branch of Indo-European developed into English, Swedish, Danish, German, Dutch, and Norwegian; from the Latin branch of Indo-European, we have modern Portuguese, Romanian, Spanish, and Italian; other Indo-European branches are Celtic (no longer spoken), Old Greek, Slavonic, Indo-Iranian, Armenian, and Albanian. Basque is considered a pre-Indo-European language because it is not related to any of the Indo-European families. It is considered an **isolate** and the only pre-Indo-European language still spoken today in Europe.

Linguists often compare two languages in an attempt to prove both their relatedness and the cultural relatedness of the peoples who speak them. If two languages share a feature (a sound, **morpheme**, or lexical item) and the presence of this feature cannot be explained by language universals, typology, or borrowing from one language to the other, historical linguists assume that the feature was inherited by both from a parent language. Therefore, a genetic relationship is established by comparison of certain linguistic features in the two languages. This method, which consists of the reconstruction of an ancestor language from the evidence that remains in daughter languages, is called *comparative reconstruction*. Indo-European is a good example. Even though no written records of the ancient Indo-European language exist, examination of certain linguistic features in languages belonging to the Indo-European family allows linguists to reconstruct it with a high degree of certainty.

Many scholars formulated theories that tried to link Basque to other languages by way of linguistic comparison. Apart from Aquitanian, which, as you read in the previous chapter, is considered to be an old form of Basque, Iberian has been the language most often related to Basque. The Basque-Iberian hypothesis states that Basque is the only descendent of a language spoken in the whole Iberian Peninsula before Romanization. The Iberos were thought to be the first inhabitants of Spain, and the Basques were believed to be their direct descendants. Supporters of the Basque-Iberian hypothesis have argued that the area where Basque was spoken in the past was geographically close to the area where we suppose that Iberian was spoken. In addition, Iberian has been shown to have a similar inventory of sounds to Basque's. However, geographical closeness and having similar sounds may just be a coincidence: Languages in contact do not have to be genetically related, and totally unrelated languages often have similar inventories of sounds since the phonetic possibilities available to speakers are quite limited.

BASQUE has also been related to Caucasian languages. This doesn't take into account the consideration that Caucasian languages belong to different families and not to a single one; the probability of finding similarities by chance among more than two families increases. African and Uralic languages have also been compared unsuccessfully to Basque. As pointed out by Trask and Jacobsen in several publications (see Required Readings), the similarities discovered are too insignificant to provide conclusive evidence of direct relationship. The so-called similarities are often based on comparison with Modern Basque lexicon; borrowings from third languages, especially Romance languages; **neologisms**; Basque modern dialectal **variants**; misguided analysis; and artificial morpheme boundaries when analyzing Basque.

Comparison is not restricted to language. Frequently, scholars compare ethnographic aspects as well, in an attempt to link different groups of people to a common ancestor.

IMPORTANT CONCEPTS

Language universals: Basic principles that govern the structure of all or most languages. Universals express what is possible in language structure.

Typology: A way of classifying languages that share structural characteristics.

Lexico-statistics: Comparison of lists of words in two languages. By examining the proportion of similarity between the pairs, linguists try to show a common ancestry between the language pair studied. Nevertheless, we should not consider similarity produced by chance.

Borrowing: A linguistic form incorporated into the system of a language from another language.

Lesson three

LEARNING OBJECTIVES
1. Introduce the objectives and methodologies of comparative linguistics.
2. Provide an overview of some theories that genetically link Basque to other languages.

3. Assess the failure of scholars to provide evidence of the genetic relations between Basque and other languages, such as Caucasian and African.

REQUIRED READING

Jacobsen, W. H. 1999. "Basque Language Origin Theories," in W. A. Douglass et al. (eds.), *Basque Cultural Studies*, 27–43. Reno: Basque Studies Program.

Trask, R. L. (n.d.d) "Prehistory and Connections with Other Languages":
http://www.cogs.susx.ac.uk/users/larry/basque.prehistory.html

Trask, R. L. 1997. "Connections with Other Languages: Summary" and "The Alleged Influence upon Castilian Spanish," in Trask, *The History of Basque*, 411–29. London and New York: Routledge.

SUGGESTED READING

Trask, R. L. 1997. "Connections with Other Languages," in R. L. Trask, *The History of Basque*, 358–411. London and New York: Routledge.

Mitxelena, K. 1988. "Relaciones de parentesco de la lengua vasca," in *Sobre Historia de la Lengua Vasca, Anejos del Anuario del Seminario de Filología Vasca* "Julio de Urquijo" 10: 56–73. The text was written in the 1960s.

WRITTEN LESSON FOR SUBMISSION

1. Basque, like English, is full of Latin words. See, for example, Basque luma, dorrea, aingerua and English paternal, decade, angel, verb. How would you counter the argument that English or Basque is a daughter language of Latin?

2. Why do you think so many scholars have tried to make a historical connection between Basque and

other languages? Why are we all supposed to be con-
nected anyway? What do you make of the similarity
in the construction of ancient pyramids in Egypt and
Mexico, for instance? Can we rely on architectural or
linguistic similarities to defend a common origin for
all humans?

4 · A Formal Description of Basque

SEVERAL characteristics of Basque make it clearly different from Indo-European languages: Basque is a morphologically **ergative language, head-final,** and highly **agglutinative.** In what follows, the main characteristics of its phonetics, phonology, morphology, syntax, and lexicon are described briefly.

THE SOUNDS

Differing from English, examination of sounds and spelling conventions in Basque shows few discrepancies. Most dialects of Basque only have five vowels (/i, e, a, o, u/); however, the dialect of Soule also possesses a sixth **vowel** (/ü/) and constrastive **nasalized** vowels.

With regard to **consonants,** Basque and English have a similar inventory of **stops**; Basque lacks **voiced fricatives** and **africates,** but possesses a wider inventory of sibilants than English: Basque distinguishes between a predorso-alveolar voiceless fricative and an apicoalveolar voiceless fricative, on the one hand, and an apicoalveolar voiceless affricate and a predorso-alveolar voiceless affricate, on the other, although both distinctions are neutralized in some varieties. In addition, only eastern Basque maintains aspiration. Differing from English, Basque does not have a **velar** nasal phoneme, but does possess a **palatal** nasal.

Trill rhotics (/rr/) and **flap rhotics** (/r/) only contrast intervocalically. For instance: *ere* 'also' and *erre* 'fire, to burn'. The spelling 'j' may indicate different sounds across dialects: jan "to eat" can be pronounced as a palatal (with several realizations) or as a velar.

With regard to intonation and accent, different dialects vary to a high degree, depending on four factors:

whether the system is tone or stress-based, whether the stress is distinctive, the syllable on which stress is placed, and whether the domain of placement is the stem or the phonological group. See Gaminde (1998) for a description of different Basque accent systems.

MORPHOLOGY

Clearly differing from Indo-European languages, Basque is morphologically ergative: the subject of an intransitive verb and the direct object of a transitive verb go in the absolute case, whereas the subject of a transitive verb ("A" in Aske's Table 2, p. 219) goes in the ergative case, as can be seen in (4.1.a) and (4.1.b). See the List of Abbreviations at the back of the book.

Eaxmple 4.1.a

Neska	*etxera*	*joan*	*da*
Girl: abs	house: all	go	AUX

'The girl went home'

Eaxmple 4.1.b

Neskak	*mutila*	*eraman*	*du*	*etxera*
Girl: erg	boy: abs	take	AUX	house: all

'The girl took the boy home'

Basque has fourteen phrase-final nominal cases, as shown in Table 4.1.

IN ADDITION, Basque also has many postpositions or function words such as *azpian* 'under', *inguruan* 'around', *barik* 'without', *(-ri) begira* 'looking at', *(-tik) kanpora* 'out of'.

Depending on the regional variety, different morphophonological changes occur when a declension case is added to a stem. Table 4-2 shows regional variation in this respect.

Table 4-1
Basque declension cases

Case	Definite sg
absolutive	A
ergative	AK
dative	ARI
possessive genitive	AREN
destinative	ARANTZAT
instrumental	AZ
inessive	AN
locative genitive	KO
allative	RA
final allative	RAINO
ablative	TIK
partitive	–
prolative	TZAT (indefinite only)

Table 4-2
Regional variation

		Variety
alaba + A	*alaba*	Gipuzkoan, Navarrese
	alabea	Western Bizkaian
	alabia	Gipuzkoan Bizkaian
	alabie	Eastern and Mid-Bizkaian
	alabi	Ondarroa Bizkaian
astoa + A	*astoa*	most varieties
	astua	Gipuzkoan Bizkaian
	astue	Eastern and Mid-Bizkaian

Basque's morphology is highly agglutinative and composed of many suffixes and postpositions. **Compounding** is very common. Unlike Spanish and French, and like English, there is no **grammatical gender.** Demonstratives represent three degrees of proximity, as in Spanish and in contrast to English.

VERBAL morphology is highly periphrastic. The auxiliary carries tense, mood, and agreement information, and a nonfinite form carries aspect information. Auxiliaries have traditionally been categorized by modality as either indicative, potential, conditional, or imperative. In addition, as already noted, the auxiliary can also be in the present or past, and it agrees with the arguments of the sentence in absolutive, ergative, and dative. For instance

Example 4.2
liburuak   ekarri   dizkizut
books: abs bring: asp   AUX:
                         ind-me: erg-yousg: dat-abspl
'I brought you the books'

Example 4.3
liburuak   ekarri   diezazkizut
books: abs bring   AUX:
                         pot-me: erg-yousg: dat-abspl
'I can bring you the books'

SYNTAX
In contrast to Spanish, French, and English, Basque basic word order is (S)OV. Basque is therefore a headfinal or left-branching language: modifiers precede their heads, except in the case of adjectives, which precede their nouns. For instance, examples 4.4 and 4.5.

Basque grammar
The structure of Basque is of great interest to linguists thorough the world. Several characteristics make Basque clearly different from Indo-European languages: it is a morphologically ergative language, head-final, and highly agglutinative. This photo shows different Basque descriptive grammars.

Example 4.4

Etorri	*den*	*mutila*	*nire*	*neba*	*da*
come:	AUX:	boy:	me:	brother:	IS
asp	relative	abs	poss	abs	

'the boy who just came is my brother'

Example 4.5

Jefferson	*Etxe*	*Zurian*	*bizi da*
Jefferson	house	white:	live
		iness	

'Jefferson lives in the White House'

A S CAN be seen in example 4.1.b, in contrast to English, Basque marks the subject (*neskak* 'the girl') and the object (*mutila* 'the boy') differently. Since the two arguments are marked differently and there is no risk of ambiguity, Basque allows for rather free word order, much like Old English, but in contrast to Modern English.

LEXICON

Lastly, although most Basque lexicon is non–Indo-European, it has borrowed many words from the languages with which it has been in contact. During the Romanization period, Basque borrowed Latin words, such as *luma* 'pen' and *makila* 'stick', and even words from Arabic, such as *alkondara* 'shirt'. Later, modern Spanish and French words came into the language. In areas where Basque is in contact with English, English loanwords, such as *troka* 'truck', *aiskrimia* 'ice cream', *estorra* 'store', and *frigueia* 'freeway', are also common.

With the spread of Basque in situations in which it was not previously used, many technical items have been codified with the use of Basque suffixes: for

instance, *eleduna* (*ele* 'word', *dun* suffix indicating possession, *a* determiner) 'spokesperson', *burujabetasuna*
(*buru* prefix indicating selfness, *jabe* 'owner', *tasun* suffix indicating abstractness, *a* determiner) 'independ-
ence'.

Lesson four

LEARNING OBJECTIVES
1. Get a general overview of the structure of Basque,
   especially the characteristics of Basque that make it
   differ from English and Romance languages.
2. Gain basic insight into the structure of Basque in
   order to be able to understand the linguistic phenomena discussed in subsequent chapters.

REQUIRED READING
Aske, J. 1997. "A Typological Overview of Basque," in
   *Basque Word Order and Disorder: Principles, Varia-
   tion, and Prospects*, 211–40. Ph.D dissertation. UMI:
   Univ. of California, Berkeley.
Trask, R. L. (n.d.a) "A Linguistic Sketch of Basque":
   http://www.cogs.susx.ac.uk/users/larryt
   /basque.sketch.html

SUGGESTED READING
Hualde, J. I. 1991a. *Basque Phonology*. London: Rout-
   ledge.
Hualde, J. I., G. Elordieta, and A. Elordieta. 1994. The
   Basque dialect of Lekeitio, supplements of *Anuario
   del Seminario de Filología Julio de Urquijo*, no. 34.
   Bilbao and San Sebastian: Univ. of the Basque Coun-
   try and Diputación Foral de Gipuzkoa.

Lafitte, P. 1979 [1962]. *Grammaire basque* (Navarro-Labourdin littéraire). Donostia: Elkar.

Note: Readers more interested in the formal side of Basque are referred to the webpage of the University of the Basque Country (see next heading), where Professor Laka provides a formal description of Batua grammar and many references on specific issues. Hualde et al. (1994) provides a good description of a Bizkaian variety.

INTERNET RESOURCES

Basque Sounds: http://bips.bi.ehu.es/basque/tbg.htm (on this site, featured by Professor Gaminde and members of the engineering laboratory Aholab of the University of the Basque Country, you can learn about Basque phonetics and listen to Basque sounds). Transcriptions using the International Phonetic Alphabet (IPA) are available.

Itziar Laka's Basque grammar: http://www.ehu.es/grammar/index.htm

Larry Trask's webpage: http://www.cogs.susx.ac.uk/users/larryt/basque.sketch.html

WRITTEN LESSON FOR SUBMISSION

1. Some people believe that Basque is not sophisticated enough for talking or writing about complex philosophical concepts; since it is such an old language, it cannot make technical distinctions that are easily made in English. Comment on this statement.
2. Another widespread belief is that Basque is an impossible language to learn, while English is an easy language, as proven by the millions of people who speak it. Which language, Basque or English, is easier to learn? Which linguistic level of Basque (phonetics,

morphology, syntax, or lexicon) would be easy for an English native speaker to learn? Which aspects of Basque would be difficult for a monolingual English-speaking learner?

5 · Status planning

IN PART TWO, we will address the sociolinguistic situation of Basque in recent decades, and language planning employed to reverse its minority status. As already mentioned, Basque has suffered geographic and social regression during the past centuries, a process known as *language shift*, and this provoked a popular reaction in the 1960s. The minority status of Basque has three main causes: first, the low percentage of Basque speakers; second, its restricted situational use for high functions, such as education and government; and third, a significant decrease in family transmission due not only to mixed marriages but, more importantly, to stigmatization associated with the use of Basque.

The first important movement to support the minority language started throughout the Basque Country in the 1960s. It focused on L1 (*alfabetatze* 'literacy') and L2 (*euskalduntze* 'Basquization') teaching of Basque to adults in *gaueskolas* 'night schools'. In addition, Basque started to be used as the language of instruction in primary education in *ikastolas*, or Basque full-immersion schools. Ikastolas began by teaching children in Basque in secrecy; they later became private, legal schools, and many ultimately became part of the public school system in the BAC and Navarre.

With the Spanish transition to democracy in 1977, language planning in the BAC and, to a lesser degree, in Navarre, passed largely into the hands of Basque institutions, such as the BAC, provincial, and municipal governments. In the Northern Basque Country, reversing language shift (RLS) planning continues to be done by private institutions, since Basque has no official status.

RLS planning has been conducted in three main areas: status planning, acquisition planning, and corpus planning. *Status planning*, the subject of the current chapter, refers to deliberate efforts to influence the functions that a language serves. In this respect, planners have promoted the use of Basque in situations previously restricted to Romance languages. The declaration of Basque as an **official language** in 1979 would provide local institutions with the resources necessary for assigning new high-level functions to Basque in education, mass media, and public administration. *Acquisition planning* refers to organized efforts to promote the learning of a language either as an L1 or L2 and will be discussed in Chapter 6. Considerable planning is being done to promote the teaching of Basque. Since Basque was used in few professional situations and subject to great dialectal variation, *corpus planning* was necessary in two areas. The lexicon needed to be modernized, especially in technical domains. In addition, the Academy undertook the task of codifying a new variety of Basque to be used for standard purposes. We will address corpus planning in Chapter 7.

BASQUE IS DECLARED OFFICIAL

GOVERNMENT language planning and policy began after the Spanish Constitution (1978) officially recognized multilingualism in Spain. Each autonomous community has undertaken the officialization of its own regional language. The Basque parliament declared Basque official in the Statute of Autonomy (1979), which establishes that "the Basque language, the language of the Basque people, shall, together with Spanish, be recognized as an official language in the Basque Country, and all the inhabitants of the Basque Country [BAC] will have the right to know and use both languages." They

First Basque schools
Ikastolas are primary and/or secondary education
schools where Basque is the medium of communication and instruction. This photo shows children and
teachers in the first Navarrese ikastola (1933).
Photo: Intxausti 1990.

---

also declared that Basque **public institutions** would
guarantee the use of both languages.

IN 1982, the parliament of the BAC approved the Act of
Normalization of the Basque Language (Law
10/1982). This act outlines the general planning guidelines to be followed by public institutions in the BAC in
order to guarantee the co-official status previously
granted to Basque by the Statute of Autonomy. It establishes the creation of an Advisory Board, chaired by the
president of the Basque Autonomous Community;
Basque Radio and Television; the regulation of **linguistic models** in primary education; and the Institute for
Adult Literacy and Basquization (HABE). The main goal
of all these institutions is to promote the acquisition
and use of Basque.

Although both Spanish and Basque are official languages in the BAC, the official status of the two languages is not the same in practice. The Spanish Constitution grants the *right and obligation* of all Spaniards to speak Spanish, whereas the Statute of Autonomy only establishes the *right* of Basque citizens to speak both official languages. Those who oppose the promotion of Basque frequently claim that a Basque language requirement for some civil servants is unconstitutional. They argue that knowing Basque is a right rather than an obligation, and requiring it is therefore discriminatory.

The Navarrese parliament approved a Foral (Provincial) Basque Act in 1986, with the opposition of all Basque nationalist parties. This act promotes Basque language teaching and public administration use exclusively in the province's Basque-speaking areas (the very north); it does not give official status to Basque in the areas where it has already been lost. Currently, the 1986 Foral Basque Language Act is being revised, again with the opposition of all Basque nationalist parties. As for Iparralde, the Basque language has no official recognition. Although it is used in institutions such as local media, church, and some schools, as is the case with other minority languages throughout France, there is little state support for Basque.

As already mentioned, the Act of Normalization of the Basque Language, approved in 1982 by the BAC parliament, established the outline of government planning for the promotion of Basque. It was decided that the public administration needed to be able to assist citizens in both official languages. The Act of Normalization of the Basque Language requires many civil servants to take Basque language classes. The Basque public administration is required to promote the hiring of bilinguals for a certain percentage of all open positions.

In addition, all official documents are translated into Basque and published in bilingual form.

With the creation of Basque Radio and Television (EITB), Basque was also introduced into the mass media. The presence of Basque in the mass media has increased its social prestige and lexical modernization. Currently, apart from EITB, a daily newspaper (Berria, former *Euskaldunon Egunkaria*) and several magazines (such as *Argia*) and journals (for instance, *Jakin*) are published in Basque. An increasing number of local magazines, radio stations, and television stations also use Basque.

THE MOST recent government step to increase the status of Basque is the General Plan for Promoting Basque Language Use (1998). This plan stresses cooperation between government and nongovernment initiatives in the promotion of Basque language use in a wide number of situations, including family transmission, youth networks, leisure activities, business, and industry. After concentrating on corpus and acquisition planning, which will be explained further in the next two chapters, RLS planning is now focusing on promoting daily use of Basque in private and public situations. In Chapter 11, we will address the General Plan for Promotion of Basque Language Use in more detail.

In addition, private groups, such as *Euskal Herrian Euskaraz* (EHE) 'The Basque Country in Basque', *Euskal Kultur Batzarrea* (EKB) 'The Congress of Basque Culture', and local groups such as *Arrasate Euskaldun Dezagun* (AED) 'Let's Basquisize Arrasate', also work to promote the status of Basque by trying to change social attitudes. Recently, a nongovernment initiative to promote the normalization of Basque, called *Euskararen Kontseilua* 'The Basque Language Committee', has gathered together fifty-seven cultural and research associations.

IMPORTANT CONCEPTS

Reversing language shift (RLS) refers to language planning efforts aimed at recovering the vitality of a language. According to Fishman, RLS is a call for not only the recovery of the language, but also cultural reconstruction and greater cultural self-regulation (1991: 17).

The term *normalization* refers to the spread of Basque language knowledge, use, and corpus. It is often used in the same sense as RLS in minority situations, such as the Basque one.

Diglossia: The minority status of Basque with respect to Spanish or French is often described as a diglossic situation by Basque language supporters. Ferguson (1959) described the concept of diglossia in the context of internal variation within a language. One variety (H) is used for the high functions of the language and another (L) for the low functions. However, scholars in minority language situations adopted the concept of diglossia to refer to the imbalance in the functional allocation of two languages. In this respect, it is often noted that the relationship between Basque and French or Basque and Spanish is diglossic because the former is hardly ever used in situations that stress status.

The term *Euskalduntze* 'Basquization' refers to the teaching of Basque as a second language.

Alfabetatze 'Literarization' of native speakers who never had formal instruction in Basque.

Lesson five

LEARNING OBJECTIVES

1. Assess government and nongovernment status planning from the creation of ikastolas and gaueskolas to the legalization of Basque and the promotion of Basque language use in institutional settings.
2. Be aware of legal regulations protecting Basque.
3. Examine basic areas of government intervention.

REQUIRED READING

Fishman, J. 1991. "The Cases of Basque and Frisian," in *Reversing Language Shift: Theoretical and Empirical Foundations of Assistance to Threatened Languages*, 149–86. Philadelphia: Multilingual Matters.

Basque Government. 2000. "Legal Status," in *Report on the Language Policy in the Basque Autonomous Community*, 14–27.

———. 2000. "The Language Policy of BAC," in *Report on the Language Policy in the Basque Autonomous Community*, 38–63.

SUGGESTED READING

Sánchez Carrión, J. M. 1991. *Un futuro para nuestro pasado. Claves para la recuperación del Euskara y teoría social de las lenguas*. San Sebastian: Seminario de Filología Vasca Julio de Urquijo and Adorez eta Atseginez Mintegia.

INTERNET RESOURCES

Official site of the Deputy Ministry for Language Policy (Hizkuntza Politika Sailburuordetza) of the Basque Government: http://www.euskadi.net/euskara/indi-cei_i.htm

Basque Radio and Television homepage: http://www.eitb.com/english

Berria, the only newspaper entirely published in Basque, has a reduced version translated into English: http://www.berria.info/english/azala.php

A weekly magazine entirely published in Basque (only in Basque): http://www.argia.com

Homepage of Euskal Herrian Euskaraz, an activist association supporting Basque monolingualism in the Basque Country (only in Basque): http://ehe.euskalerria.org/sarrera.cfm

Euskararen Kontseilua homepage (association in favor of Basque): http://www.kontseilua.org

WRITTEN LESSON FOR SUBMISSION

1. The United States has no official language. English is the national language, and some people have requested its officialization. A few states have passed laws to make English the only official language in their state. Write a position paper advocating the officialization of English in the United States. Give clear arguments for such an important measure.
2. Defend the opposing position.
3. Compare the possible officialization of English to the officialization of Basque.

6 · Acquisition Planning

THE FIRST efforts to promote Basque language use during the Franco regime were in popular acquisition planning through the creation of *ikastolas* and *gaueskolas*. In ikastolas, children could use Basque as the medium of instruction. In gaueskolas, adults could learn Basque as either their first or second language. These initial efforts were characterized by their activist, popular nature. At a time when the Basque language was persecuted, it acquired great symbolic value as an ethnic and nationalist marker, and even a sign of contesting the dictatorship. With the legalization of Euskara in the Southern Basque Country and the beginning of government activity in support of it, acquisition planning fell to the Basque government. In Iparralde, private associations have long been engaged in acquisition planning, the most important being *Seaska*, the association of ikastolas in Iparralde. In addition, the French public education system allows a bilingual program called *Ikasbi* in some schools.

The ikastolas developed the Model D (full immersion in Basque) of the primary education system. The other two linguistic models in use are Model A, in which Spanish is the language of instruction and L2 Basque is taught for a few hours a week, and Model B, a bilingual program. Parents decide which model they want for their children's education. As shown in Graph 6-1, an increasing number of parents favor Basque full-immersion education.

Since students usually complete their education in the same linguistic model with which they started, by examining the changes in enrollment percentage across levels of education, we can observe longitudinal trends.

Graph 6-1

Enrollment in infant and primary education in 1998–1999

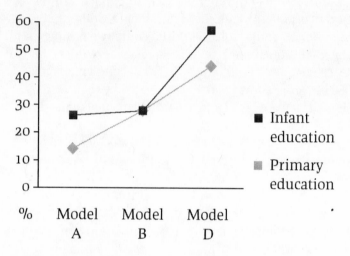

Model D on the rise
Basque families choose more and more the Basque model of education (model D) for their children.
Adapted from Basque Institute for Statistics, July 23, 1998

The data presented in Graph 6-1 indicate a clear increase in the number of children enrolled in immersion Basque (Model D) programs during recent years. Only 44% of the children currently enrolled in Primary Education chose Model D, whereas more than 57% of the children currently enrolled in Infant Education chose Model D. In other words, more parents are now enrolling their children in the Basque monolingual program than a decade ago. In a parallel trend, there is a clear decrease of children enrolled in monolingual (Model A) Spanish programs (26.61% in Primary and 13.93% in Infant Education), whereas the percentage of students enrolled in bilingual programs (Model B) remains about the same (29.37% and 28.66% respectively). These data show the high value that Basque society is giving to the acquisition of the Basque language.

ON THE other hand, the fact that the number of children enrolled in bilingual programs is not increasing may reflect a general concern over Basque language proficiency. Several studies on children's linguistic proficiency in Basque and Spanish have showed that Model D students have good command of both languages, whereas Model A and Model B students are proficient in Spanish but not in Basque (Azurmendi, 1983; Etxeberria, 1987; Etxeberria and Aierbe, 1988; Elosua et al., (1994). Moreover, by age twelve even Model D students scored significantly better in Spanish than in Basque. Since Basque is spoken by only one-third of the population, it is difficult for children living in non–Basque-speaking areas to fully acquire it. By contrast, the wider diffusion of Spanish, as a result of both the two languages' situational distribution and the higher number of Spanish speakers, makes this language easy to learn. Since Spanish can be learned easily by social interaction, many families feel that it is better for their children to use Basque in school as much as possible. The high number of very young children enrolled in Model D proves this tendency.

The euskaldunization of the education system required a prior euskaldunization of teachers, which was established as a priority by the Basque government. Large amounts of money were allocated to the *Irale* program to fund language classes, and even paid leaves-of-absence for teachers so they could gain proficiency in

Late literacy
'Alfabetatze,' literacy in their own native language, was
necessary for Basque speakers. The Labayru Institute
has been teaching Basque language and literature
classes to Biscayan adult native speakers since 1970.
Photo from Euskararen Berripapera 26.

Basque. As a result, the percentage of teachers in the
public system who have mastered Basque rose from 5%
for the 1976–1977 academic year to 65% during
1998–1999.

GOVERNMENT planning also supported language
learning for civil servants in an attempt to guarantee citizens linguistic rights. A percentage of all public
positions are assigned a language requirement that
varies in proficiency level, depending on the type of job.
Greater proficiency is demanded of employees in more

technical or higher-level positions than of those in non-technical positions. The percentage of positions requiring Basque proficiency varies according to the sociolinguistic situation in the community affected: Highly bilingual areas require a greater percentage of bilingual positions in public administration.

LASTLY, the following private groups in favor of the normalization of Basque also contribute to acquisition planning at varying educational levels: *Alfabetatze eta Euskalduntze Koordinakundea* (AEK) 'Association of Basquization and Literarization' and *Labayru Ikastegia* 'Institute Labayru', among others, teach Basque to adults; *Ikastolen Konfederakundea* (IK) 'Association of Ikastolas' is engaged in primary and secondary education; and *Udako Euskal Unibertsitatea* (UEU) 'Basque Summer University' teaches university-level courses entirely in Basque.

Lesson six

LEARNING OBJECTIVES
1. Examine language planning in the teaching field, including child and adult education.
2. Learn about primary education linguistic models: monolingual and bilingual education.
3. Introduce nongovernment and government acquisition planning.

REQUIRED READING
Fishman, J. 1991. "The Cases of Basque and Frisian," in *Reversing Language Shift: Theoretical and Empirical Foundations of Assistance to Threatened Languages*, 149–86. Philadelphia: Multilingual Matters.

Basque Government. 2000. "Legal Status," in *Report on the Language Policy in the Basque Autonomous Community*, 14–27.

Basque Government. 2000. "The Language Policy of BAC," in *Report on the Language Policy in the Basque Autonomous Community*, 38-63.

SUGGESTED READING

Etxeberria, F. 1999. *Bilingüísmo y Educación en el País del Euskara*, 89–226. Donostia: Erein.

Sánchez Carrión, J. M. 1991. *Un futuro para nuestro pasado: Claves para la recuperación del Euskara y teoría social de las lenguas*. San Sebastian: Seminario de Filología Vasca Julio de Urquijo and Adorez eta Atseginez Mintegia.

INTERNET RESOURCES

HABE homepage: http://www.habe.org/habenet /principal_i.htm

AEK homepage (only available in Basque and Spanish): http://www.aeknet.net

Department of Education, Universities, and Research of the Basque Government (only available in Basque and Spanish): http://www.euskadi.net/entesinstitu-cionales/hezkuntza/indice_i.htm

Labayru Ikastegia homepage: http://www.labayru.com

Association of Ikastolas homepage: http://www.ikastola.net

Udako Euskal Unibertsitatea homepage (only available in Basque): http://www.ueu.org

Mendebalde Kultur Alkartea (an association of scholars that promotes the corpus and status of Western Basque and its contribution to Batua) homepage (only available in Basque): http://www.mendebalde.com

Table 6-1
Senate Bill No. 88, State of Nevada (January 10, 1995)
THE PEOPLE OF THE STATE OF NEVADA, REPRESENTED
IN SENATE AND ASSEMBLY, DO ENACT AS FOLLOWS:
Section 1. Chapter 388 of NRS is hereby amended by
adding thereto a new section to read as follows:

1. The board of trustees of each school district shall,
   subject to the approval of the state board, establish a
   program to provide for the bilingual education of
   pupils with limited proficiency in the English language.
2. The state board of education shall adopt regulations
   which are necessary to administer and carry out such
   a program.
3. As used in this section, "pupils with limited proficiency in the English language" means those pupils
   whose:
   (a) Primary language is not English;
   (b) Proficiency in the English language is below the
       Haverage proficiency of pupils at the same age or
       grade level whose primary language is English;
       and
   (c) Probability of success in a classroom in which
       courses of study are taught only in the English
       language is impaired because of their limited
       proficiency in the English language.

After reading Senate Bill No. 88, of the State of Nevada,
consider the following questions:

1. Compare bilingual education promoted by the
   Basque Government and bilingual education in the
   American context as represented by Senate Bill No.
   88 of the State of Nevada reproduced in Table 6-1.

What are the similarities and/or differences in the objectives of the Basque and Nevada policies supporting bilingual education?

2. To whom is bilingual education directed in each case?

3. What are the social implications of bilingualism in the two cases?

4. What are the difficulties faced by planners in the Basque and American cases?

5. Take a position on the policy of spending public money to promote bilingual education in each of the two cases. Give convincing arguments for or against such a measure.

7 · Corpus Planning
The Codification of Batua

CORPUS planning has been extremely important in the case of Basque, because of a nearly universal lack of literacy in the minority language until recent times. Since written Basque was highly restricted and Basque was not used in most formal situations, it lacked many resources available to normalized or majority languages. If Basque was to be used in education, mass media, and public administration, it needed modernization—in other words, the codification of a new lexicon. Private institutions, such as UZEI, Elhuyar, and UEU, have worked on this codification.

In addition, great dialectal variation (see Chapter 12) and the lack of a standard and written tradition made the creation of a unified variety for standard purposes necessary. In 1976, Euskaltzaindia, the Basque Language Academy, decided to give priority to the study and codification of Basque grammar, designate style norms, and promote Batua.

THE CODIFICATION OF BATUA
The Academy of the Basque Language was created in 1918 with three main objectives: to regulate spelling, to codify new lexicon, and to enhance literary Basque. It took the members of the Academy a long time to decide, however, whether to promote an existing geographical dialect as the literary variety or to create a new one with elements of various dialects. This discussion was controversial in the early twentieth century, and traces of the opinions articulated then are still evident today.

Interesting proposals surfaced before the decision about the nature of the literary variety was made. One of these proposals was *Gipuzkera Osatua* 'Enhanced

Gipuzkoan'. Bizkaian linguist and Academy member Azkue proposed the use of Gipuzkoan as the basis for literary Basque, using the other dialects to enhance it. Since Gipuzkoan is geographically central, it was thought to be the easiest for speakers of other dialects to understand. Azkue had practical reasons (mutual intelligibility) to propose Enhanced Gipuzkoan as the variety that should be promoted.

Another proposal that influenced the development of Batua was the use of *Lapurtera Klasikoa* 'Literary Labourdin'. Its advocate, Krutwig, offered political reasons for establishing a unified variety as the national language. Although Krutwig's proposal was not fully accepted, three of his points influenced the creation and development of Batua. First, he established the main criterion of *correct usage* by promoting the idea of *literary tradition*: forms that appear in the literary tradition are automatically accepted as correct. Second, he also stressed the need for making Basque a *culture language* and modernizing its lexicon. Third, he stressed the idea that Batua needed to be spread throughout the Basque Country and become the *national language*. This idea was taken by the more radical nationalist, who often proclaimed: *"herri bat, hizkuntza bat"* ('one nation, one language'). Although Krutwig's proposal was not adopted, the three criteria of literary tradition, culture language, and national language remain influential.

THE PROPOSAL ultimately adopted embraced both Krutwig's Literary Labourdin and Azkue's Enhanced Gipuzkoan. Following Krutwig, it was based on the idea of literary tradition. Following Azkue, it was also based on central dialects. Gipuzkoan had been perceived favorably historically; it is the most central dialect, and therefore easier for most people to understand than any other; and, as observed by Azkue, Gipuzkoan has a high

EUSKALTZAINDIA

Euskaltzaindia
In order for the Basque language to be used in a wide variety of formal situations, it needed to undergo a process of standardization. Following the Spanish and French models, the Academy of the Basque Language, Euskaltzaindia, was created in 1918.

---

number of Basque speakers (almost 40% of all those in the Basque Country), and is not surrounded by Romance languages. Many claim that it has undergone fewer linguistic changes and is, therefore, less "polluted" than other varieties.

The codification of Batua started with unified spelling norms. Verbal morphology was also a great concern from the outset, since Basque has a rich auxiliary system and, although the same information is encoded in all dialects, the morphemes vary. Auxiliaries mark person, number, and tense. For example, the verbal auxiliary in the sentence 'I brought them to you' takes different morphemes in several dialects, as shown in example 7.1 (see the List of Abbreviations at the back of the book).

Example 7.1
Gipuzkoan and Batua:
ekarri d-izk-i-zu-t:

D	I	ZKI	ZU	T
AUX:	root of verb	pl obj -	you:	me:
pres-	*izan-*		dat-	erg

'I brought them to you'

Bizkaian:
ekarri d-eu-tsu-da-z:

D	EU	TSU	DA	Z
AUX:	root of verb	you:	me:	
pres-	*eutsi-*	dat-	erg-pl obj	

'I brought them to you'

Navarrese:
ekarri d-erau-zki-tzu-t:

D	ERAU	ZKI	TZU	T
AUX:	root of verb	obj pl-	you:	me:
pres-	*eraun-*		dat-	erg

'I brought them to you'

This multidialectal form illustrates variation in the root (*-i-*, *-eu-*, *and* *-erau-*), the pluralizer of the direct object (*-zki-*, *-z*), and the dative morpheme (*-zu-*, *-tsu-*, *-tzu-*). As in example 7.1, mostly Gipuzkoan verbal forms were chosen for Batua.

More recently, pronunciation and lexicon are being codified. The criterion for the former is historical: older phonemes are favored, for instance, the palatal over the velar in words like *jan* 'to eat', which is produced with a palatal [yan] in Navarrese and many Bizkaian varieties and a velar [xan] in Gipuzkoan and some Bizkaian varieties.

WITH RESPECT to codification of lexicon, the Academy established two main criteria for selecting one particular lexical variant over others. On one hand, forms with a written tradition and those currently in use are favored. On the other, French and Spanish borrowings are disfavored.

The Academy has not addressed the situational distribution of Batua. Only in 1998, when suggestions on pronunciation were published, did the Academy explicitly address situational variation. The Cultivated Pronunciation of Euskara Batua (CPEB) (Euskaltzaindia, 1998) is to be used for "cultivated speech," and "formal speech" (literally, 'speech of high level'). CPEB represents the standard oral language and is supposed to be used for the formal functions of the language, such as news broadcasting, public speeches, lectures, and school (literally, "for explanations in school"). CPEB does not need to be used in informal situations or when dialects are used.

The Basque situation is rather unusual in that standard ideology (***prescriptivism***) does not come from a group of otherwise similar social characteristics. The suggestions made by the Academy affect a high number of people because Basque is a minority language and Basque society accepts RLS planning. Teachers, professors, journalists, and editors, among others, take these suggestions seriously, although this does not necessarily mean that they follow them. Today, acceptance of

Batua is fairly pervasive; although many speakers feel that regional dialects also need to be promoted. During the past few years, the "one nation, one language" idea has lost support even among many radical nationalists, and manifestations of dialectal pride, especially in Bizkaian-speaking areas, are on the rise.

Lesson seven

LEARNING OBJECTIVES
1. Assess the role of the Academy in the standardization and modernization of Basque.
2. Learn about the codification of Basque technical lexicon and the work conducted in the field by institutions such as UZEI, UEU, and Elhuyar.
3. Situate the codification of a new standardized variety (Batua) in the context of a minority situation.
4. Apply the one nation, one language idea to the promotion of Batua.
5. Critically assess arguments for and against the codification and promotion of a unified variety.
6. Raise questions about prescriptivism; consider several definitions of correctness.

REQUIRED READING
Finegan, E. (n.d.) "What Is 'Correct' Language?" Language Society of America (LSA) webpage: http://www.lsadc.org/Finegan.html
Haugen, E. 1997 [1966]. "Language Standardization," in N. Coupland and A. Jaworsky (eds.), *Sociolinguistics: A Reader and Coursebook*, 341–52. Hampshire and London: MacMillan.
Rodríguez, F. 1993. "Unity of the Basque Language and Basque Political Unity," originally published in

Basque in Uztaro 9, translated by Alan King:
http://ibs.lgu.ac.uk/forum/Iborn.htm

Urla, J. 1993a, "Contesting Modernities: Language Standardization and the Making of an Ancient/Modern Basque Culture," *in Critique of Anthropology* 13(2):101–18.

SUGGESTED READING

Zuazo, K. 1988. *Euskararen Batasuna*. Bilbao: Royal Academy of the Basque Language.

INTERNET RESOURCES

Euskaltzaindia (Basque Language Academy) homepage:
http://www.euskaltzaindia.net

UZEI homepage: http://www.uzei.com

Euskalterm database (a database of technical lexicon; you can do searches of Basque lexicon items in English after registering to enter the online database with a free subscription):
http://www.www1.euskadi.net/euskalterm
/indice_i.htm

WRITTEN LESSON FOR SUBMISSION

1. Explain the differences between dialect and language.
2. Explain the four aspects of language development proposed by Haugen. Apply Haugen's categories to the Basque case.
3. In most societies, the definition of correct usage is associated with who uses the particular linguistic form (see Finegan on LSA webpage), so that forms used by powerful groups are usually recognized as "correct" forms. How does linguistic ideology promoted by Euskaltzaindia differ from the idea of correct usage in American society?

8 · The Current Situation
Basque Language Knowledge, Use, and Attitudes

A S NOTED in previous chapters, an important characteristic of Basque society is bilingualism. Only about one-third of the BAC population is bilingual, however. In what follows, a description of language knowledge, use, and attitudes for the Basque-speaking portion of the population will be provided. Table 8-1 shows language competence in the Basque Autonomous Community.

The percentage of Basque speakers varies by province: Gipuzkoa has the highest percentage and number of Basque speakers (bilinguals), about half its population, whereas less than one-quarter of Bizkaians speak Basque, and not even 15% of Arabans do so. The high number of quasi-Basque (incomplete) speakers also stands out—almost half a million, or one-fifth of the total population of the Basque Autonomous Community. This group, together with that of non-natives who are fluent Basque speakers, is quantitatively significant. Such individuals could also be influential in language change since they are likely to produce transfer from Spanish. Lastly, Basque monolingualism is a characteristic of the past. Only a few older people cannot speak Spanish. By contrast, half of the BAC's population is Spanish monolingual.

The percentage of monolingual non–Basque-speaking population is lowest in the French Basque Country. The number of Basque speakers there is only about 70,000, and the percentage of Basque speakers is much lower in the younger generations. Although 45% of those older than sixty-four are Basque speakers, only 20% of those from sixteen to twenty-four know Basque. Such figures

Table 8-1
Language competence in the BAC
according to the 1996 Census

	Monolingual Spanish	Balanced Bilinguals	Quasi-Basque	Total
Araba	182,166	40,479	54,366	277,011
	65.76%	14.61%	19.63%	100%
Bizkaia	622,266	266,107	233,227	1,121,600
	55.48%	23.73%	20.79%	100%
Gipuzkoa	214,467	330,230	119,217	663,914
	32.30%	49.74%	17.96%	100%
BAC total	1,018,899	636,816	406,810	2,062,525
	49.40%	30.88%	19.72%	100%

*Adapted from Basque Institute for Statistics webpage,
July 23, 1998*

demonstrate a dramatic decrease in Basque knowledge
in just two generations. Nevertheless, a small but ardent
group of people is working to promote the use of Basque
in schools.

NAVARRE is home to the highest percentage of
monolingual non-Basque speakers. This is not surprising, given that local Basque is spoken only in the
northernmost area. The number of new acquirers is
slowly increasing in other areas of the province, however. Contrary to the decreasing numbers in the French
Basque Country, the percentage of Basque speakers in
Navarre remains fairly constant across generations
(from 10 to 15%), and more and more families are
enrolling their children in education programs with
Basque as the or one of the languages of instruction.

LANGUAGE USE

Historically, use of Basque has been restricted until recently to informal situations involving family and friends, and religious services. With the beginning of reversing language shift planning and policy, the use of Basque started to spread to formal situations, such as education, mass media, and government encounters. The use of Basque remains low in these venues, however. Basque usage in industry, most private services, and health and judicial services is even lower.

Although about one-third of the BAC population identifies itself as bilingual (see Table 8-1), the actual use of Basque is even lower in both formal and informal situations, and in most geographic areas. Bilingual citizens reported speaking more Basque within the family, with children's teachers, with priests, and in the market, whereas use of Basque is minimal when interacting with bosses and health-care providers. Basque has traditionally been spoken in tight local networks, such as the family and neighborhood, and church institutions. Use of the language in professional settings remains low despite RLS efforts, because high mobility results in intense contact with Spanish speakers.

ANOTHER study measured the use of Basque longitudinally with a different methodology (Altuna, 1998). This series of measurements of Basque use was conducted in urban settings at four-year intervals beginning in 1989. Researchers walked down the street at the same time, in different towns, recording the language being used by the groups of speakers within earshot. Even though judgments might have been subject to variation, this indirect measurement provides interesting data. The study showed that the *use* of Basque is lower than directly reported *knowledge*, even in the settings where use of the minority language is more likely

We know Basque, why not use it?

Many people may know a language but speak it hardly
ever. In fact, although about one-third of the BAC population identifies itself as bilingual, the actual use of
Basque is much lower in both formal and informal situations, and in most geographic areas.

Photo by Josu Amuriza.

Graph 8-1
Use of Basque in informal urban situations

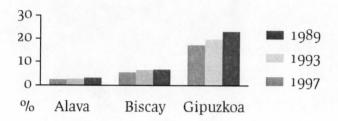

Increasing use of Basque
Increase in the use of Basque in the last years is only remarkable in Gipuzkoa, the province where the use of Basque is largest.
Adapted from Altuna, 1998: 22

to occur—during informal interactions with friends and relatives. Graph 8-1 shows the percentage of informal social encounters conducted in Basque in the BAC provinces in the three successive measurements.

As THE data show, Basque is not widely used in urban settings—even in Gipuzkoa, the province with the highest number of Basque speakers. We can also observe a slight increase from 1989 to 1997, but this increase is only substantively significant in Gipuzkoa (from 17.02% to 19.65% to 22.91%). Use of Basque in Araba increased less than 1% during the period in question (from 2.04% to 2.56% to 2.93%); in Bizkaia, it increased just over 1% (from 5.39% to 6.21% to 6.56%). When the claimed language competence percentages (Table 8-1) are compared to the language use figures (Graph 8-1), it is clear that even in Gipuzkoa, the

province with the highest number of Basque speakers
(50%), only about 20% of informal conversations were
actually conducted in Basque.

This incongruity between language knowledge and use
has several explanations. The high number of monolingual Spanish speakers and Basque speakers of limited
proficiency makes interaction in Basque difficult. In
addition, many Basque speakers shift to Spanish even
when all conversationalists know Basque because its
minority status and previous stigmatization make some
speakers reticent to use it in public. Finally, many
young speakers who only speak Batua switch to Spanish
in informal settings because they only master a formal
register of Basque, which may not be perceived as appropriate or functionally useful in colloquial situations.

IDENTITY AND ATTITUDES TOWARD BASQUE LANGUAGE PROMOTION

Any planning aimed at producing social change needs
to take the community's attitudes toward the given government intervention into account. Attitudes and identity issues are especially important in minority language
promotion. The value of the given language in a community's identity determines their attitude toward government intervention in its favor.

THERE IS no consensus on the importance of
Basque's role as an integrative element of Basque
identity. According to the Basque Government (1996),
44% of the population throughout the Basque Country
has a favorable or very favorable attitude toward planning promoting Basque, and 18% has an unfavorable
or very unfavorable attitude. Those in favor of RLS
planning tend to be Basque speakers and to give political and cultural reasons for learning Basque, whereas
those opposed to such planning who learned Basque as

a second language reported instrumental motivations for doing so. We will address the differences between people who define their ethnicity as Basque and those who do not in Chapter 24.

Lesson eight

LEARNING OBJECTIVES
1. Get a general sense of the sociolinguistic situation of Basque in terms of language knowledge, use, and attitudes.
2. Assess quantitative differences in the degree of bilingualism across regions.
3. Pay attention to differing definitions of Basque identity.
4. Identify attitudes toward promotion of the Basque language.

REQUIRED READING
Basque Government. 1996. *Sociolinguistic Study of the Basque Country 1996: The Continuity of Basque 2*, 1–49. Vitoria-Gasteiz: Basque Government Press.

SUGGESTED READING
Altuna, O. 1998. "Euskararen kale erabilpena Euskal Herrian," *Bat Soziolinguistika Aldizkaria* 28: 15–64. Quantitative measurement of Basque language use in public informal settings in towns with over 10,000 inhabitants.
Erize, X. 1997. *Nafarroako Euskararen Historia Soziolinguistikoa 1863–1936*, 321–64. Iruña: Navarrese Government Press. Sociolinguistic situation of a Navarrese town, using qualitative methods (group discussions). There is a shorter Spanish version available,

also published by Navarrese Government Press (*Historia Sociolingüistica de Navarra: 1863–1936*).

WRITTEN LESSON FOR SUBMISSION
Study the sociolinguistic situation of the BAC town of your choice. Provide a diagnosis of the situation in terms of demography, language knowledge and use, and any other language-related features. Use the database of the Department of Language Policy of the Basque Government and any other information you can find on the Internet or at the Basque Library at the University of Nevada, Reno. The database, which is composed of data reported in the census, is available online at the following address: http://www1.euskadi.net/euskara_soziolinguistika/indice_e.htm.The database is only available in Basque. The notes and translations in the following chart should be sufficient to enable you to use it. All data can be retrieved in both absolute numbers and percentages. You can also get the software to give you charts (grafikoak). The database offers information classified in seven areas.

Table 8-2
Notes and translations for using the Department of Language Policy's database

1. Population: 1996, by age groups
2. Language Competence (5 years old or older): 1981–1996. The language competence categories are the following:
   euskalduna   Basque-speaker
   elebidun hartzailea   Incomplete bilingual
                                  (incomplete in Basque)
   erdaldun elebakarra   Spanish monolingual
3. Mother Tongue (5 years old or older): 1986–1996

4. Language used at Home (5 years old or older): 1996

euskara	Basque
euskara eta gaztelera	Basque and Spanish
gaztelera	Spanish
beste	other

5. Native Language Competence (5 years old or older): 1986–1996

euskaldunzaharrak	native Basque-speakers
jatorrizko elebidunak	native bilinguals
euskaldunberriak	non-native Basque-speakers
partzialki euskaldunberriak	incomplete non-native Basque-speakers

6. Language used at home by language competence: 1991–1996

euskaldunzahar aktiboak euskaraz	active Basque natives in Basque
euskaldunzahar aktiboak bietan	active Basque natives in both languages
euskaldunzahar pasiboak euskaraz	passive Basque natives in Basque
jatorrizko elebidun aktiboak euskaraz	native active bilinguals in Basque

7. Language used at home by density of Basque-speaking networks (5 years old or older): 1996.

9 · Linguistic Attitudes: Indirect Methods

ATTITUDES toward Basque and Spanish have been addressed through direct and indirect methods. In the previous chapter, we addressed identity and attitudes toward promotion of Basque language use, as measured by government language planners through direct questioning. In this chapter, we will examine attitudes toward Basque dialects, Batua, and Spanish, gathered through indirect methods.

Indirect measurement methods are more reliable than direct questioning because people often report what they believe they are supposed to think, or, in other words, what is socially acceptable, rather than what they really think about something. When they do not know that they are being observed, speakers give subconscious reactions that better reflect their true social attitudes.

Speaker attitudes need to be taken into consideration before making any attempts at language planning, because the disadvantaged situation of a minority language is not likely to be reversed if speakers do not have a positive attitude toward the variety devised. In addition, educators, sociologists, psychologists, and sociolinguists are very interested in pinpointing linguistic attitudes and their causes because of the potential social consequences of stereotypical negative attitudes. In the Basque case, the study of attitudes toward Basque and Spanish can show people's predisposition toward accepting RLS planning and policy. Moreover, the study of dialectal attitudes can shed light on the future of regional dialects and the social acceptance of Batua.

The method most frequently used to collect linguistic attitudes indirectly is the *matched guise* technique

(MG). The MG technique was first used in the 1960s by Lambert and his associates in a study measuring Canadians' reactions to French and English. Bilingual speakers recorded the same passage in both languages, a practice that was a means of collecting attitudes toward speakers of French and English among both Francophones and Anglophones. The results showed great stigmatization of French even, and especially, among French speakers. Not only did French speakers rate speakers more negatively when they spoke French than when they spoke English, but they also perceived the French guises more negatively than did English speakers.

The MG technique was then used in numerous studies, most often together with the *semantic differential* (SD) technique. The SD is a measurement scale that designates the opposing extremes of a trait, such as "smart," "hardworking," or "good-hearted." The traits are used to measure different aspects or dimensions of attitudes that can be corroborated with statistical techniques such as Principal Components Analysis.

TWO BASIC dimensions underlie many aspects of social interaction. Along a status dimension, subjects evaluate speaker competence: their intelligence, self-confidence, and so forth. Along a solidarity dimension, subjects evaluate speakers in terms of social attractiveness, in other words, in qualities important in a solidarity-stressing situation, such as generosity and sociability. Socially stigmatized groups are often perceived by the in-group negatively (as less competent) along the status dimension, but positively (as more friendly) along the solidarity dimension. These two dimensions coincide with the notions of *overt* and *covert prestige* in variationism (Trudgill, 1974) and *instrumental* and *integrative motivations* (Gardner and Lambert, 1972: 14) in second-language learning.

Once the ratings given to each speaker of a matched guise in each dimension have been calculated, we can compare the means given to the guises. By performing analyses of variance (ANOVAs), we can show that the means are statistically significant, or in other words, that speakers are perceived differently whether they use one variety or another.

TWO STUDIES have examined attitudes toward speakers of Basque and Spanish using matched guises. A study conducted during the 1980s among high school students learning Basque (Echano, 1989) showed no strong stereotypes toward Basque or Spanish speakers. Instead, Echano stresses the "overall acceptance of speakers of both languages in terms of likability or status without any significant discriminatory image which could reach a level to establish the existence of a self-diminishing image by some speakers or even a compensatory one in terms of Social Attractiveness to make up for a situation of weakness in social status" (1989: 353).

As perceived by high school learners of Basque, the Basque situation during the 1980s was one of settling more than one of conflict: Echano did not find strong stereotypes toward Basque or Spanish despite the clear minority situation of Basque. At that time, Basque had just been declared official, and one might have expected a more positive reaction toward Basque speakers at the affective (solidarity) level to balance its lower status.

A more recent study using the matched guise technique (Amorrortu, 2000a) among university bilingual students did not find strong stereotypes associated with speakers of the different Basque and Spanish varieties either, although it did find some differences. Batua was not recognized as a variety more prestigious than the others. Rather, students from Bizkaian-speaking areas favored Bizkaian speakers over their Batua guises in

How do you like us?
When using an indirect method to gauge attitudes, we keep the subjects from realizing that their linguistic attitudes are being investigated. Linguistic attitudes, especially subconscious reactions, are crucial because they may influence language behavior.
Illustration by Seymour Chwast.

both solidarity and professionalism (or status). As expected, since Gipuzkoan and Batua are linguistically close, speakers of these varieties were not evaluated differently. In addition, students evaluated Spanish less favorably than Basque along the professionalism dimension, but equally in terms of solidarity. Lastly, perceived proficiency in Basque was closely associated with professionalism, so that less proficient speakers were perceived by all groups as less professional than Spanish speakers but equally attractive along the solidarity dimension. Only low-proficiency speakers of Basque (speakers with clear L2 features) were clearly disfavored along the professionalism dimension; they were not, however, disfavored along the solidarity dimension.

THE REPORTED results have consequences for RLS planning. The lack of preference toward Basque speakers along the solidarity dimension points to the need to stress integrative motivations for learning and using the minority language. Since the situational distribution of Basque is clearly less widespread than is that of Spanish, and since bilingual speakers are in the minority, unless Basque speakers perceive Basque as an important part of their identity, they might be inclined to turn to Spanish in their more intimate relations.

IMPORTANT CONCEPTS

Direct and *indirect* methods in the measurement of linguistic attitudes: When using a direct method to measure linguistic attitudes, we ask our subjects their opinion about a language variety directly in a questionnaire or interview. When using an indirect method, we keep the subjects from realizing that their linguistic attitudes are being investigated.

Figure 9-1
Example of semantic differential scale

good ___ ___ ___ ___ ___ ___ ___ bad
    3   2   1   0   1   2   3

Dimensions: *Status* (professionalism) and *solidarity*, *overt* and *covert prestige, instrumental* and *integrative* motivations to learn a second language. The status aspect of social interaction is characterized by demonstrable influence, power, and control; the solidarity aspect is attributed to a person who is similar to the speaker, and is associated with frequent interaction and intimacy. Trudgill coined the terms *overt* and *covert* prestige to address the same dichotomy in variationist sociolinguistics. Varieties have overt prestige when they are those of speakers who are in power. This prestige is conscious. Varieties are covertly prestigious when, despite social stigmatization, their speakers accept them at the affective or integrative level. Similarly, instrumental motivations for learning a second language (to get a better job, for instance) stress the status aspect, whereas integrative motivations (to be part of a group, for example) stress the solidarity one.

The *matched guise technique* is an experimental method to uncover linguistic attitudes. The MG technique controls all variables except language in an attempt to ensure that the attitudes are given toward (speakers of) the varieties rather than other variables, such as the voice quality of the speaker or the topic of the speech sample. The same bilingual or bidialectal speaker produces the same oral text in two or three varieties. In order to avoid recognition of the guises' voices as belonging to the same person, the recordings are ordered in such a way that listeners hear filler voices in between the guises. Since the respondent does not know that the speaker of the guises is actually the same, if the attitudes toward the two MGs are different, it can be concluded that the attitudes are caused by the variety used in the guises.

Semantic differential scale. The SD is a technique frequently associated with the use of the MG. A scale designates opposite extremes of a trait, for instance Figure 9-1.

Reliability of the measurement of attitudes: *Principal Components Analysis* (PCA). Solidarity and professionalism are two constructs that need to be measured with multiple indicators that ensure high reliability (that is, ensuring that they are actually measuring the same concept). PCA is a multivariate analysis technique of data reduction. This technique reduces the number of variables (indicators—in this case, personality traits) that explain the distribution of the data, by clustering together those that behave similarly. Rather than assuming the attitudinal dimensions and the personality traits that can measure them, PCA gives evidence that the indicators of those constructs are valid (that is, reliable).

Lesson nine

LEARNING OBJECTIVES
1. Consider direct and indirect methods for collecting linguistic attitudes.
2. Identify dimensions in linguistic attitudes.

3. Consider social and educational consequences of linguistic attitudes.
4. Explore attitudes toward Basque and Spanish.
5. Learn about attitudes toward regional dialects of Basque and Batua.

REQUIRED READING

Amorrortu, E. 2000a. *Linguistic Attitudes in the Basque Country: The Social Acceptance of a New Variety*, 1–10, 205–22. UMI: Univ. of Southern California.

Milroy, L., and D. Preston. 1999. "Introduction," *Journal of Language and Social Psychology* 18(1): 4–9.

SUGGESTED READING

Amorrortu, E. 2001a. "Métodos indirectos en la medición de actitudes lingüísticas: El euskara frente al castellano," in A. I. Moreno (ed.), *Perspectivas Recientes sobre el Discurso/Recent Perspectives on Discourse*. Servicio de Publicaciones de la Universidad de León y Aesla: León.

———. 2001b. "Unibertsitate-ikasleen euskalki eta batuarekiko jarrerak," in *Mendebaldeko Euskal Kultur Alkartea, Euskalkia eta Hezkuntza*, 61–80. Bilbao: Mendebalde Euskal Kultur Alkartea.

Echano, A. 1989. *Attitudes toward Euskera: Using the Matched-Guise Technique among School Children in the Basque Country*. Unpublished dissertation, Univ. of Edinburgh.

Edwards, J., and H. Giles. 1984. "Applications of the Social Psychology of Language: Sociolinguistics and Education," in P. Trudgill (ed.), *Applied Sociolinguistics. London*: Academic Press.

WRITTEN LESSON FOR SUBMISSION

1. Discuss some advantages and disadvantages of direct and indirect methods of collecting linguistic attitudes.

2. Do you think that the fact that a study on linguistic attitudes uses direct or indirect methods may change the results? Why or why not?

3. Do you think that a positive attitude toward a certain linguistic variety necessarily implies a wider use of that variety? In other words, does a positive attitude toward Basque among Basque-American Basque speakers, for instance, necessarily imply use of Basque? Why or why not?

4. What are some of the possible social and educational consequences of speaking a socially stigmatized variety? Think, for example, of an African-American or Hispanic-American youth. What are the social and educational consequences of learning a variety close to the standard in the given community at home? Think, for example, of a middle-class child from Boston going to school in her neighborhood.

10 · The future of Basque
Evaluation of RLS Planning

TWO DECADES of government RLS planning in the
Basque Country have produced some changes.
According to the Basque Institute for Statistics, from
1986 to 1996, the percentage of Basque speakers
increased from 24.58% to 30.88% (Eustat website, July
23, 1998). However, these data must be taken with caution. On one hand, the census collects self-reported data,
which are not always totally reliable. On the other hand,
proficiency has not been objectively measured, and
"speaking well" probably does not mean the same to
everybody answering a census questionnaire.

In any case, in the BAC, where the majority of planning favoring the minority language has been conducted and its situation is better, the increased status of
Basque is obvious; it is now serving more functions than
ever before, as can be seen in linguistic landscaping,
mass media, public administration, and the education
system. Nevertheless, it is not obvious that the status of
Basque has improved notably in other areas. Use among
youths, especially non-natives, and in the judicial system, business and industry, for instance, has not
improved.

We can describe government planning and policy in
the Basque Autonomous Community as promoting the
learning of Basque for instrumental reasons. Some criticism has been directed toward the general approach for
promoting Basque taken by the Basque government.
According to Fishman (1991), RLS planners should first
concentrate on teaching the minority language as an L2
and on promoting family transmission. They should
then introduce the minority language: first into primary
education, later into the work environment and into

mass media, and, finally, into the government. This process can be described as a bottom-up approach to RLS. Fishman criticized government language planning because it promoted the status of Basque in the educational system, mass media, and the government, and did not pay enough attention to family transmission (1991: 158–82).

Language planning has focused to differing degrees on status-stressing and solidarity-stressing motivations for the use of Basque at different times. Language planning began privately with the creation of *ikastolas* and *gaueskolas* in the 1960s, stressing identity (integrative) reasons for learning and using Basque. At the time, when Basque had no official recognition and its use was prohibited, the reason to maintain or even learn it as a second language was not to gain upward mobility. There were no instrumental reasons; rather, the use of Basque showed solidarity and a desire to integrate into the Basque-speaking community.

WITH THE onset of democracy and the institutionalization of Basque language planning, the Basque and local governments valued Basque knowledge and promoted instrumental motivations to learn it. Research has shown that instrumental motivations may be enough to encourage out-group members to learn the minority language. However, economic incentives (the possibility of promotion or getting a job in a government institution, for instance) do not guarantee proficiency, especially in the case of speakers who do not feel that this language is an essential part of their ethnicity. Martínez-Arbelaiz's article (1996) reports on the failure of many civil servants to pass a standardized Basque-language test even when the Basque government subsidizes all expenses in the teaching process.

Lately, the Plan of Normalization of Use has returned to placing a stress on the solidarity (identity, integrative) aspect of language. This plan has promoted knowledge and, more importantly, use of Basque, in formal and intimate situations alike.

ON THE other hand, policymakers are known for the quantitatively oriented nature of their concerns. The main concern of language planners has been to increase the percentage of Basque speakers. Language specialists and laypeople alike widely believe that the fact that an individual reports a speaking ability in a language, or even passes a standardized test, does not guarantee *communicative competence* in or use of the language. Official reports on the number of Basque speakers need to be taken with caution, since they do not guarantee wider use of Basque.

Many reasons may cause new acquirers not to use Basque. They may not be participants in Basque-speaking networks, or they may disfavor its use for personal reasons, for example, if they learned it for exclusively instrumental reasons. In addition, despite possessing a command of grammar and written or even oral skills in formal (that is, school-like) settings, a new learner may not have the communicative competence needed to successfully speak Basque in a wide range of situations. Many Basque scholars have shown concern for what they often call, stressing Spanish transfer, "the quality of Basque."

It is true that many Spanish speakers are learning Basque either as adults or as children; what needs to be examined is whether these students acquire enough communicative knowledge to use the language in a wide range of situations. A further stress on the integration of L2 speakers into the Basque linguistic community

Family transmission

Most experts agree that the future of a language depends largely on family transmission, in other words, in passing the language from parents to children. Ahoz aho, belaunez belaun 'From mouth to mouth, from generation to generation' is the logo used in a consciousness-raising campaign held by the Basque Government.

would guarantee improved communicative competence and wider use of Basque in everyday situations.

LASTLY, it is often claimed that, as in biological life, when a language is in danger of disappearing, only intervention can ensure the reversal of the trend. Language planners often point to their work to account for Basque's relatively good situation in the BAC vis-à-vis

that in Iparralde or Navarre. In fact, the future of Basque
seems more positive in the BAC than in other areas.
Taking a great number of sociodemographic and sociolinguistic variables into account, a simulation model
indicates dramatic language shift in Iparralde, maintenance in Navarre, and improvement in the BAC (Garaialde et al., 1998). The resulting data must be taken with
caution, due to the assumptions built into the model's
design and the variables unaccounted for (such as the
possible effect of migration trends, tourism, and even
the current, highly controversial political situation).
Nevertheless, even the most optimistic forecasts foresee
a very negative future for the Basque language in Iparralde.

DIFFICULTIES IN LANGUAGE PLANNING

1. A great obstacle can arise because part of the community may not experience the minority language as
   part of their identity. Frequently, this part of the community does not feel that public funds should be
   used to promote the minority language.
2. Exclusively instrumental reasons for learning a
   minority language: If learners have only instrumental
   reasons, it will be difficult to stimulate the use of the
   minority language.
3. Giving quantitative results priority over qualitative
   results: What about communicative competence? The
   main objective of language planners is to get larger
   numbers of speakers. Qualitative issues, such as communicative competence, often become a secondary
   concern.
4. How can family transmission be planned? Most
   experts agree that the future of a language depends
   largely on family transmission, which is the most difficult area for government intervention.

Lesson ten

LEARNING OBJECTIVES

1. Critically evaluate language planning in primary education and public administration.
2. Be aware of predictions for the future of Basque.

REQUIRED READING

Garaialde, I., et al. 1998. "Modeling the Long Term Future of the Basque Language," 1–15. Paper presented at the *Basques in the Contemporary World: Migration, Identity, and Globalization* Conference, Reno.

Martínez-Arbelaiz, A. 1996. "The Language Requirement Outside the Academic Setting: The Case of the Basque Administration," *Journal of Multilingual and Multicultural Development* 17(5): 359–72.

SUGGESTED READING

Larrañaga, I. 1998. "Euskararen Egoerari Buruzko Iker-ketak: Euforia-Giroa eta Konfusio-Zeremonia," *Zenbat Gara Bizitza eta Hizkuntza Aldizkaria*, no. 3: 18–31.

INTERNET RESOURCES

Basque Institute of Statistics webpage: http://www.eustat.es

WRITTEN LESSON FOR SUBMISSION

1. Critically evaluate the claim that the status of Basque is better in the BAC because of government intervention.

2. Based on your findings from your study at the end of Chapter 8 on the sociolinguistic situation of a town in the Basque Country, consider a few suggestions you might make for the city council board. Assuming that politicians want balanced bilingualism in their town, what measures would you suggest to be taken to achieve that goal?

11 · **Promoting Basque language use**
A General Plan

THE GENERAL Plan for Promoting Basque Language Use, discussed for the different domains of use by several language experts, was approved by the Basque Government in 1998. Most language planning to be carried out in the BAC in the coming years will be configured by the guidelines listed in this plan. The plan's main objective is to decide on and promote the planning measures necessary to guarantee both the linguistic rights of Basque speakers and the survival and normalization of Basque. In essence, the plan's aim is to increase use of Basque in different domains. The plan places special emphasis on the following concepts: *communicative competence*, since use of a language is determined by speakers' ability to communicate successfully across a wide range of situations; and, *linguistic networks*, since the absence of minority speakers in specific situations, and even the presence of a few monolinguals, causes a reduction in the chances of speaking Basque.

Creators of the plan reported the positive and negative aspects of the current situation of Basque in different domains, before proposing specific areas for further promotion. Rather than completing an in-depth assessment of the specific measures already implemented, language planners noted the advantageous status of Basque in the BAC in comparison to Iparralde, concluding that government language planning and policy is the reason for this difference. In fact, the diagnosis of the situation made in the first part is not supported with quantitative data, and therefore appears superficial and even impressionistic. The diagnosis is also very vague in the assessment of what issues are problematic, such as the "ideology problem" of some euskaltegis (43–44).

Despite the problems already noted, the plan gives us the chance to identify the linguistic issues currently of concern to scholars and language experts. The following issues are worth emphasizing:

1. "The quality of language" (36, 41): A concern for Basque proficiency shown in citations of Spanish transfer at the phonetic and grammar levels (40); citations of family varieties as more "natural" (63)— other varieties thus being "artificial"; need to improve proficiency among teachers and broadcasters (63). In essence, despite the quantitative increase in the number of bilingual speakers through the years, the authors of the plan report a concern on the quality of Basque being used, which is often characterized as "artificial" and full of transfer from Spanish.

2. The functional allocation of different Basque varieties: Citations of the use of dialects (37, 55) and the undue weight of Gipuzkoan varieties (40). The experts complaint that little attention is being paid to regional varieties and that Gipuzkoan varieties, linguistically closer to Batua, are often used as the standard.

3. The undue weight of written over oral registers (40): A concern on the overuse of linguistic strategies generally characteristic of written registers even in oral registers, which produces a kind of oral discourse too elaborated.

4. Making speaking Basque as useful and rewarding as speaking Spanish (52). This concern points to the low number of speakers having a high degree of identification with the Basque language (lack of the integrative aspect), which often causes them to switch to the majority language.

Basque in the work environment
Use of Basque in the work environment and technology
is rather low. Language experts who participated in the
General Plan for Promoting Basque Language Use
(1998) highlight the need for Basque to be
promoted in those areas.
Photo from Euskal Etxeak 48

The Plan also points to some objectives for the
future: First, experts stress the necessity of continu-
ing promoting the transmission of Basque, through
family transmission, the linguistic levels of primary
education, and literacy and L2 teaching to adults.
Second, they highlight the need for Basque to be
promoted in areas such as technology, the work
environment, leisure activities, religion, the public
administration, and areas with a high density of
Basque speakers. Third, the quality of Basque needs
to be improved (corpus planning) in the media,

advertising, publishing, and cultural activities in general. We can expect that most promotion of Basque will be done in the mentioned areas.

Lesson eleven

LEARNING OBJECTIVES

1. Become acquainted with the plan that will guide most institutional language planning in the Basque Country in the years to come.
2. Critically evaluate the plan and previous government planning.
3. Identify experts' concerns in what respects the current status and future of Basque.

REQUIRED READING

Basque Government. 1998. *General Plan for Promoting Basque Language Use*. Vitoria-Gasteiz: Basque Government.

WRITTEN LESSON FOR SUBMISSION

1. What are the strategic fields of action of the General Plan for Promoting Basque Language Use?
2. What are the fields in which language planning have not had desirable results, according to the experts who worked on the plan?
3. One of the principal components of government language planning is positive discrimination. According to the Basque government (1998: 25), "if the aim is to redress existing inequality [between Basque and Spanish], you cannot apply the same language policy to two languages in different situations. If two languages are left to their own devices or just simply left as they are, the gap between the stronger and the weaker will widen, to the detriment of the weaker.

Therefore, language policy must be directed at assisting the weaker language, the one which is used in more restricted environments, but without this affecting the basic rights of people." Evaluate the concept of positive linguistic discrimination and compare it to positive discrimination policies favoring ethnic and other minorities (women, for instance) in the United States. Also consider the egalitarian ethos present in both the American and Spanish constitutions. How can we reconcile positive discrimination favoring minority access to resources with the idea that everybody should be treated equally in a democratic system?

12 · **Regional Variation**

T HE BASQUE language exhibits great regional variation. Although the dialects were linguistically closer
earlier in history, lack of literacy in Basque and communication among speakers of different regional varieties
produced intense change in the different varieties. The
first detailed classification of Basque regional dialects
was made by Prince Bonaparte in 1863. Basque dialectol-
ogist Zuazo updated Bonaparte's classification in 1998.
Figure 12-1 shows Basque regional varieties.

Among the dialects, those at the periphery—Bizkaian
(Western varieties) and Souletin—differ notably from
the others. Bizkaian is spoken in the province of Bizkaia,
northern Araba, and Western Gipuzkoa (as far as the
Deba River). There are two main Bizkaian subvarieties:
Eastern Bizkaian (which includes Gipuzkoan Bizkaian)
and the variety of Markina and Western Bizkaian (which
includes the rest of varieties spoken in Bizkaia).

Bizkaian is characterized by linguistic changes in the
final vowel of a stem when the determiner is added. For
instance,

Example 12.1

alaba + A:	*alabea:*	Western Bizkaian
	alabia:	Gipuzkoan Bizkaian
	alabie:	Eastern and mid-Bizkaian
	alabi:	Ondarroa Bizkaian

Another characteristic of Bizkaian is the neutralization
of **sibilants.** For instance, Bizkaian speakers produce
atso 'old lady' (apicoalveolar voiceless affricate in other
dialects) as *atzo* 'yesterday' (predorso-alveolar voiceless
affricate), and *zu* 'you singular' (predorso-alveolar voice-

Table 12-1
Number of speakers of each dialect
(adapted from Yrizar, 1981: 214–15)

Dialect	Speakers	Percentage
Bizkaian	200,400	37.56
Gipuzkoan	200,100	37.5
Low Navarrese	46,500	9.71
High Navarrese	51,600	9.66
Labourdin	23,000	4.31
Souletin	11,100	2.08
Unknown	800	0.14
Total	533,500	100

less fricative in other dialects) as *su* 'fire' (apicoalveolar voiceless fricative).

IN NOUN morphology, the sociative case is formed by adding -*gaz* instead of the more common -*rekin*: for instance: *aitagaz* (*aitarekin*) 'with the father'. Bizkaian also differs from the other dialects in that placement of stress distinguishes the singular from the plural, as shown in example 12.2.

Example 12.2
gizónak 'the man' / *gízonak* 'the men'

Verbal morphology also varies across regions, especially with respect to auxiliaries. For instance, Bizkaian *ekarri deutsut* 'I brought you something' from root **eutsi* and more common *ekarri dizut* 'I brought you something' from root **i*.

On the other hand, Souletin differs from the other Basque dialects in having a sixth vowel (ü), nasal vowels, and aspiration, among other linguistic characteristics.

Basque Regional Dialects

This map shows Basque regional dialects following Zuazo's classification. Thin lines mark provinces, thick ones show boundaries of dialects.

1. Western. Varieties of Bizkaia, Deba, and Araba
2. Central. Varieties of Gipuzkoa (except Deba), and Western Navarre
3. Navarrese. Bortzirieta, Malerreka, Baztan, Ultzama, Aezkoa
4. Eastern Navarrese. Erronkari (lost today) and Zaraitzu (almost lost)
5. Souletin. Basabürü, Pettarra
6. Labourdin and Low-Navarrese

With respect to the number of speakers, Bizkaian and Gipuzkoans are most numerous. Table 12-1 shows a simulation of the number and percentage of speakers of each regional dialect.

SOME dialects—Bizkaian, Gipuzkoan, Souletin and Navarrese-Labourdin—have a degree of literary tradition; among them, Navarrese-Labourdin has been the most prestigious and the most often used in written works. Axular's writings in seventeenth-century earned a high reputation and have influenced literary Basque into the present. In fact, Labourdin was almost the only dialect used in written literature until the eighteenth century.

During the eighteenth century, many efforts were made to codify the Gipuzkoan dialect, including Larramendi's grammar and dictionary. The Bizkaian and Souletin literary dialects would not be codified until the nineteenth century.

Historically, the most prestigious dialects have been Labourdin and Gipuzkoan. Basque literature is full of mentions of the "richness," "beauty," "comprehensibility," "authenticity," and "purity" of coastal Labourdin, Gipuzkoan from Beterri and, to a lesser degree, Bizkaian from Markina. Since Bizkaian and Souletin are the dialects that differ the most from the central varieties (that is, from Gipuzkoan and Labourdin), they also differ the most from the unified variety, and their speakers often feel frustrated by the effort they need to make to approach the standard. Currently, a rise in Bizkaian dialectal pride can be observable in the use of the regional dialect in certain public spaces formerly dominated by Batua.

Lesson twelve

LEARNING OBJECTIVES
1. Become acquainted with Basque regional variation.
2. Consider the differing historical prestige of Basque regional dialects.
3. Situate the literary dialects in their historical context.

REQUIRED READING

Amorrortu, E. 2000a. "Basque Dialectal Variation," in *Linguistic Attitudes in the Basque Country: The Social Acceptance of a New Variety*, 32–63. UMI: Univ. of Southern California.

SUGGESTED READING

Txillardegi et al. 1987. *Dialektologiaren Hastapenak*. Iruiñea: Udako Euskal Unibertsitatea.

Zuazo, K. 1998. "Euskalkiak, gaur," *Fontes Linguae Vasconum* 78: 191–233.

INTERNET RESOURCES

Bakio, Meñaka and Zamudio Basque:
http://bips.bi.ehu.es/ahoweb/en/proc.html Professor Gaminde makes available a description of several Biscayan varieties on this site (available only in Basque). You can also listen to narratives in these varieties.

Bizkaieraren fonotekea:
http://bizkaifon.ehu.es/en/html_/sarrera.html A Biscayan Sound Archive, based on Gaminde's corpora: You can listen to recordings of Biscayan varieties and read the appropriate transcriptions.

WRITTEN LESSON FOR SUBMISSION
1. Why do you think the Basque language developed so many regional dialects in such a limited geographical area?

Prince Bonaparte and Basque dialectology
Foreign scholars made Basque of international academic
concern. The first detailed classification of Basque
regional dialects was made in 1863 by Prince Bonaparte,
shown in this picture.

2. Can Basque regional dialects develop into independent languages, just as Latin became Spanish, French, and Italian? Why or why not?
3. Why are some dialects more prestigious than others are? What reasons have been given in the Basque case? Are these reasons sufficient in your opinion? Consider what you learned in Chapter 7 about prescriptivism in American society.
4. Explain the term authenticity as applied to Batua and regional varieties.

13 · Social and Register Variation

LANGUAGES are far from being homogeneous and cate-
gorical entities. In fact, as we saw in the previous
chapter, Basque has very different regional dialects. But
linguistic variation is not only due to the differences
among speakers of geographical groups. In this chapter,
we address situational and social variation. Registers or
situational varieties are language varieties appropriate
for use in particular speech situations. Registers refer to
varieties of use—in other words, varieties produced as
the consequence of different situational parameters. The
same speaker uses different linguistic forms, depending
on the situational factors of the speech situation:

1. The activity and the purpose of the activity: For
   instance, a sermon and a story told to your friends
   require different language because the two activities
   have very different purposes. The former seeks to
   teach a lesson whereas the later may just be trying to
   entertain your friends.
2. The topic: Depending on whether you are talking
   about religion or soccer, for instance, you would use
   different language.
3. The mode: Oral and written language are different;
   spontaneous speech and edited speech are certainly
   different too. Written and edited language samples
   tend to be more elaborate than oral and spontaneous
   ones.
4. The relationship among the speakers: Whether conversationalists are intimate friends or not will affect
   the way they use language; people who know each
   other well often rely on context instead of being
   explicit and elaborating their ideas.

We can mark register at all levels of language, through:

1. Lexical choice: Using or not using slang, or using hika, or forms of address, for example (See Chapter 20 for a discussion of forms of address), when appropriate according to the situation.
2. Phonological variation: Using more contractions in spontaneous intimate oral interactions and less in more formal situations.
3. Grammar: Deciding whether to use a passive rather than an active sentence, or whether to use complex subordination rather than coordination, for instance.
4. Discourse-level devices: For instance, by using certain discourse markers in informal situations, such as English *you know* and *well*, or Basque *ba* and *bueno*.

On the other hand, *dialects* are varieties characteristic of regional or social groups. Dialects have to do with *users* (groups of speakers), while registers have to do with *uses* (situations of use). British, Australian, and Boston English, on the one hand, and Souletin and Biscayan, on the other, are English and Basque regional dialects respectively. African-American Vernacular English and Hispanic English are ethnic varieties—the varieties characteristic of the African-American and Hispanic ethnic groups respectively. Likewise, the differences in speech between women and men, older and younger speakers, or educated and noneducated speakers are due to social differences between these groups. Such varieties constitute dialects.

DIFFERENCES among varieties of use and users are in most cases gradated rather than absolute, and many linguistic features are used to mark both dialects and registers. One group may use a certain linguistic feature more often than another does. For instance, less-educated English speakers may use [in] for -ing more frequently than do highly educated speakers, but at the same time, speakers of both groups use [in] more frequently in colloquial speech than in more formal situations. We may also find that contractions are used less, and passives used more, in news broadcasting than in an interview with a Hollywood star. In this case, we will find register differences.

IN BASQUE, few studies of register or social dialects have been conducted to date. In what follows, we examine the use of different registers and the varieties of different Basque-speaking groups. In a study of word order, Aske (1997) reports clear register differences between Basque oral and written speech. Using oral and written corpora of narratives, Aske found that inversions of the verb-final generalizations (SVO structures instead of SOV ones, for example) are much more common in oral speech than in written texts. For instance, in main affirmative sentences, the verb-final order in an object-verb structure is kept in 83% of the written cases, whereas in the oral corpus the same ordering of constituents was only kept in 17% of the cases.

In addition, there are also linguistic differences in word order in the speech of children and educated adults using the same register: storytelling. Although the differences between the two groups are quantitatively smaller than the differences between the oral and written registers, the adult group still used more verb-final clauses, less subject immersion, and more verb-final dependent clauses than the children.

Consideration of dialectal and situational variation is crucial when examining language change because this is never produced simultaneously and at the same rate in all groups of speakers and in all registers. In addition, analysis of linguistic variation can help avoid misconceptions, such as the idea that the external influence of another language is the only possible cause of language change—for example, the idea that the inversion of verb-final constructions among young speakers, and especially in oral speech, is produced only as a consequence of the influence of Spanish, without taking into consideration that such inversions are also common among older speakers and in written registers. In any case, the detailed examination of linguistic variation can also show that although Basque tends to be an SOV language, other word orders are also possible and not necessarily produced by the external influence of other languages.

Linguistic variation can also be examined in the context of language acquisition. Children acquire language in its social context. They not only learn a linguistic form; they also learn, at the same time, in which circumstances its use is appropriate. The ability to reproduce linguistic forms appropriately across situations is called *communicative competence* and is related to register variation.

WE CAN get children to demonstrate how they use language in different situations of use by asking them to play with puppets. If they can appropriately reproduce language playing different roles, we can note their good communicative competence. Amorrortu 2001c. reports that ten-year-old children were able to use the discourse marker *bueno* in all the functions proposed for adult speech: to accept something and to disagree, as pragmatic functions; as a transition, topic continuity and repair device, as textual functions. In addition, ten–year-olds were also aware of (and able to reproduce) the fact that higher status people, such as teachers and parents, use the discourse marker *bueno* more often. Living in a hierarchical society, children request

Social dialects

Dialects are varieties characteristic of regional or social groups. Speakers use a variety that identifies them with the group they want to belong to and, at the same time, differentiates them from other groups. For instance, older users use a variety that differs from the one used by the younger.

Photo by Josu Amuriza

---

and adults decide (accepting or partially disagreeing, as shown by the use of *bueno* in their role-playing). Those occupying higher status roles are not only the ones who accept more, but also the ones who structure the sequential development of conversation more often, as perceived and reproduced by children.

Lesson thirteen

LEARNING OBJECTIVES
1. Consider social and situational variation: dialects and registers.
2. Become acquainted with Basque dialectal variation due to age differences.
3. Learn about the situational parameters that determine register variation.
4. Inquire about acquisition of register variation: the acquisition of Basque communicative competence.

REQUIRED READING

Amorrortu, E. 2001c. "The Discourse and Social Use of DM Bueno in Eight- and Ten- Year Old Basque-Speaking Children," in M. Almgren et al. (eds.), *Research on Child Language Acquisition*. Proceedings of the8th Conference of the International Association for the Study of Child Language, 250–63. Somerville, MA: Cascadilla Press.

Aske, J. 1997. "Characteristics of the Corpus," in *Basque Word Order and Disorder: Principles, Variation, and Prospects*, 261–88. Ph.D dissertation. UMI: Univ. of California, Berkeley.

SUGGESTED READING

Finegan, E., and D. Biber. 1994. "Register and Social Dialect Variation: An Integrated Approach," in D. Biber and E. Finegan (eds.), *Sociolinguistic Perspectives on Register*. New York: Oxford Univ. Press.

WRITTEN LESSON FOR SUBMISSION
1. Explain communicative competence, and give two examples in English.

2. Explain the differences between dialect and register, and give two examples of each (not those mentioned in the chapter text).
3. Why is slang a situational variety and not a dialect?
4. Although Basque has great regional variation, it has not developed (or at least maintained) a very rich range of registers and social dialects. Why do you think the previous statement may be true? If so, do you think the minority status of Basque could have something to do with the lack of register and social variation? Could Basque social organization peculiarities have promoted reduced social variation? Why?

14 · Structural Language Attrition

Hizkuntza bat ez da galtzen
ez dakitenek ikasten ez dutelako
dakitenek erabiltzen ez dutelako baizik.

*'A language does not disappear because those who do
not know it do not learn it but because those who know
it do not use it.'*

—Artze

LANGUAGE contact situations usually result in language shift. When monolingual speakers are exposed to the culture of more powerful people, the former often try to adapt to the powerful group. Learning the language of the other is crucial for this purpose. Whether speakers learn the second language for integrative (to integrate into the new culture) or instrumental (to gain social mobility) purposes, the result is a bilingual situation that likely develops into language shift for the accommodating group. When this shift happens, speakers use their native language in a decreasing number of contexts, and this reduced use produces erosion of their linguistic skills in their first language. First, speakers lose register variation; later, the structure of the native language begins to reflect language change, often in the form of simplification or reduction.

Children growing up bilingual may not acquire both languages at the same level, and their linguistic competence in the language they use less may be reduced. Both incomplete acquisition and language loss are attrition phenomena, and it is often difficult to distinguish which of the two is more responsible for language change.

Likewise, it is important to define the linguistic proficiency level of bilingual speakers. *Full speakers* are fully proficient speakers and serve as models of comparison with *semispeakers*. The latter are recognized as not having a good command of the language ("not speaking well") by full speakers. Although usually able to communicate in the weak language, they speak a variety that differs considerably from that of full speakers. *Terminal speakers* are far along in the process of language loss, and although they can remember words and produce simple sentences, they are not able to fully communicate in the given language.

Language proficiency categories (that is, full speakers, semispeakers, and terminal speakers) are broad and difficult to apply in an empirical study. In the Basque case, since Basque is a minority language, almost all of its speakers are bilingual. Many, especially in the younger generations, are more proficient in Spanish or French, so it is difficult to point to full speakers. Before investigating any specific linguistic phenomenon in a subject's speech, it is, therefore, very useful to establish a proficiency continuum along which s/he is locatable. Placing subjects along a proficiency continuum does not solve the problem of defining who is fully proficient. It does, however, allow us to assign relative proficiency levels more objectively. If our subjects are classified beforehand by proficiency level, we can examine the use of any linguistic feature in speakers with differing proficiency levels. We can also investigate the degree of loss of certain linguistic features, and make predictions about the kinds of linguistic phenomena likely to occur among speakers sharing linguistic characteristics (for instance, proficiency) and social characteristics(for example, amount of language use, or social networks).

There are several ways to define linguistic proficiency. Some linguists assume that loss of lexicon is parallel to syntactic attrition, and they measure linguistic proficiency using common vocabulary tests. Subjects who score the highest in a translation of common vocabulary are considered the ones with the greatest linguistic proficiency, whereas those who score lowest in the lexicon test are considered the ones with the least proficiency.

Scholars placing more importance on social aspects classify their subjects according to language use. Speakers claiming to use the language under study in a wide range of situations are considered full speakers, and speakers reporting reduced use are considered semi-speakers.

HOWEVER, the best way to define a linguistic proficiency continuum is through a combination of both linguistic and social criteria, since the two are not always directly related. Modern statistical techniques, such as Factor Analysis, allow the researcher to cluster speakers who have similar linguistic proficiency based on both social criteria (self-reported use of the language in different situations, for instance) and linguistic criteria (the use of a relevant linguistic feature).

As already noted, the primary cause of language attrition is the lack of use of a language—generally because another language is used instead. When examining structural attrition, however, we need to distinguish between linguistic change produced as a consequence of universal tendencies in language loss and change produced as a consequence of transfer of structures present in another language.

The debate between defenders of *external influence* and defenders of *internal causes* is crucial in the field of language change in contact situations. Some linguists claim that languages are totally *permeable* and, there-

Incomplete acquisition
Children growing up bilingual may not acquire both
languages at the same level, and their linguistic competence in the language they use less may be reduced.
Dover Pictorial Archive.

---

fore, transfer can occur at any level of language (Thomason and Kaufman, 1988). Others, in contrast, do not
believe that it is possible to transfer syntactic structures
(Silva-Corvalán, 1994; Landa and Elordui, 2000).

SOME RESEARCH has been conducted on structural
language loss in Basque. In this chapter, we focus
on several compensatory strategies used by Basque
semispeakers as a consequence of language attrition.
Drawing from data provided by semispeakers in Bizkaia
and Nevada, Elordui (1999) concludes that the influence
of Spanish and English on the linguistic changes found
is only indirect: When there is a parallel structure in
both languages, structural ***permeability*** from Spanish
and English into Basque is a possibility. Rather than

---

adopting a structure from the other language, speakers relax a restriction present in Basque, so the external influence can only be considered indirect.

S PEAKERS have several strategies to cope with linguistic limitations due to reduced use of Basque. One such strategy is to generalize simple structures already present in the language, such as periphrastic (rather than synthetic) forms. The easiest example is the extended use of periphrastic auxiliary potential forms, such as regional variants:

Example 14.1
Eastern: *egiten ahal dut*   'I can do it'
Western, Central: *egin ahal dut*   'I can do it'

instead of:

Example 14.2
Western: *egin neike*   'I can do it'
Central: *egin dezaket*   'I can do it'

Example 14.1 illustrate the use of particle *ahal* to make the potential with an indicative auxiliary verb, instead of the appropriate potential specific auxiliary shown in example 14.2.

Past, example 14.4, and subjunctive forms are often substituted for forms based on the present, example 14.3, and indicative, respectively. For example:

Example 14.3
Western: *esan deustazun*   'you told me'
(present auxiliary form + N: past morpheme)

instead of:

Example 14.4
Western: *esan zeustan*   'you told me'
(past auxiliary form)

In Chapter 18, we will address other cases of linguistic simplification in situations of reduced use.

Lesson Fourteen

LEARNING OBJECTIVES
1. Explore language loss and structural attrition.
2. Consider incomplete acquisition.
3. Situate speakers in a proficiency continuum: full speakers, semispeakers, terminal speakers.
4. Differentiate internally and externally motivated language change.

REQUIRED READING
Elordui, A. 1999. "Processes of Language Shift and Loss: Evidence from Basque," in *Studies in Multilingualism*. Tilburg: Univ. Press.

SUGGESTED READING
Landa, A., and A. Elordui. 2000. "Sobre las gramáticas bilingües y la permeabilidad estructural," in *Estudios de Lingüística Inglesa Aplicada*.
Silva-Corvalán, C. 1994. *Language Contact and Change: Spanish in Los Angeles*. Oxford: Clarendon Press.
Thomason, S. G., and T. Kaufman. 1988. *Language Contact, Creolization, and Genetic Linguistics*. Berkeley: Univ. of California Press.

WRITTEN LESSON FOR SUBMISSION

1. Explain why is it important to establish a proficiency continuum before studying any linguistic phenomena in contact situations.
2. Explain linguistic permeability.
3. Compare the concept of linguistic permeability with that of cultural permeability. Are cultures also permeable? If so, are they permeable at all levels? Can any cultural value or trait be borrowed? Why or why not?

15 · Bilingualism

TRADITIONALLY, languages have mostly been examined in isolation, especially by linguists. However, as Romaine (1996: 573) has observed, bilingualism—and even multilingualism—is the norm, not the exception, throughout the world. In a time when high technology and worldwide communication are prominent in our lives, contact between different cultures and languages is becoming more intense. Throughout history, Basques have been in contact with several peoples and, consequently, with several different languages. Part Two of this book deals with several social and language planning issues related to the current bilingual situation in the Basque Country. In Part Three, we are focusing on linguistic variation and, now specifically, on variation produced in language contact situations outside the Old country. Before getting into contact varieties of Basque in the following chapters, we will stop and consider several issues related to bilingualism.

Many scholars are interested in bilingualism. Traditional linguists were interested in language contact only from a historical linguistics point of view, and frequently considered varieties characteristic of contact situations to be deviant or imperfect. Linguists today, however, especially sociolinguists, conduct research in bilingual situations focusing on both linguistic and social issues and without doing deficit-based types of analysis of bilingualism phenomena. Some of the topics examined in language contact situations include linguistic transfer and borrowing, communicative competence, language competence measurement, code switching, language attrition, and bilingual first-language acquisition.

The study of language also reveals social and cultural traits of speakers. By examining language, we can better understand social and cultural relationships between groups of people. Sociologists focus on topics such as minority language situations, reversing language shift planning and policy, differences between bilingualism and diglossia, and differences between individual and social bilingualism. Social psychologists and sociologists study linguistic attitudes in order to examine intergroup relations. Bilingual situations also reflect interesting ethnolinguistic identity issues.

IMPORTANT CONCEPTS

Social bilingualism and *individual bilingualism*: Broadly speaking, bilingualism is defined as the ability to speak two languages. However, not all individuals in bilingual societies are bilingual. Very often, more than one language is official in a country, but not all individuals are multilingual. For instance, although there are four official languages in Switzerland, bilingualism— and even multilingualism—while common, is not universal. The concept of *social bilingualism* refers to a community in which two languages are spoken. The term *individual bilingualism* refers to the ability of a person to speak two languages.

ANOTHER important issue is the *degree* to which an individual is bilingual. Some authors believe that full or balanced bilingualism is impossible because one of the languages will always be stronger than the other one; no one uses two languages exactly the same way in all the same situations (see description of *diglossia* below.)

Transfer was defined by Weinreich (1974) as "the incorporation of language features from one language into another with the consequent restructuring of the sub-systems involved." Another term frequently used is *interference*, which also refers to the influence of one language on another. A *borrowing* is a form of direct transfer. For example, American Basque *lontxea* is a borrowing from English *lunch*, and has been adapted to the morphophonology of Basque.

Communicative competence is a term coined by Hymes (1972) as a reaction to Chomsky's linguistic competence (see definition below).Communicative competence entails the knowledge not only of grammatical rules, but also of social and cultural rules. According to this conception, real (not idealized) speakers master a language when they know how to use it—how to distinguish the appropriate use of certain linguistic forms.

Linguistic competence: Knowledge of the grammatical rules of a language by an idealized speaker.

Code switching: The use of two or more languages in the same speech turn. Code switching can be used situationally—as a marker of style in certain situations—by balanced bilinguals, or it can be a compensatory strategy for unbalanced bilinguals with reduced communicative competence in one of the languages.

Structural language attrition: Erosion or loss of certain linguistic structures as a consequence of reduced use. Attrition is characterized by loss of lexicon and morphology, simplification, and reduction of linguistic rules.

Diglossia and *bilingualism*: Ferguson (1959) described the concept of *diglossia* in the context of internal variation within a language, where one variety is used for the high functions of the language (H) and another is used for the low functions (L). Fishman revised Ferguson's

Speaking more than one language
Bilingualism and even multilingualism is the norm,
not the exception, throughout the world.
Illustration by Jennifer Vega.

concept of diglossia, stressing the difference between
diglossia and bilingualism. *Diglossia* refers to the distribution of more than one language variety to serve different communicational tasks in a society, whereas *bilingualism* refers to an individual's ability to use more
than one language variety. In minority situations, the
term *diglossia* is often used to refer to a situation in
which one language is widely used in situations stressing status, while the other is used in a reduced number
of situations.

THE *Sapir-Whorfian hypothesis:* Language is not just
the instrument for voicing ideas, but is itself the
shaper of ideas. Whorf defined two important principles.
The principle of *linguistic determinism* states that how

one thinks is determined by the language one speaks. The principle of *linguistic relativity* states that differences among languages must therefore be reflected in the differences in the worldviews of their speakers.

Lesson fifteen

LEARNING OBJECTIVES

1. Understand basic concepts related to bilingual situations before getting into the Basque case.
2. Compare bilingual issues in the American and the Basque contexts: social bilingualism, individual bilingualism, and degrees of bilingualism; diglossia and bilingualism; and language-contact phenomena, such as linguistic transfer.

REQUIRED READING

Romaine, S. 1996. "Bilingualism," in W. C. Ritchie and T. K. Bhatia (eds.), *Handbook of Second Language Acquisition*, 571–604. San Diego: Academic Press.

WRITTEN LESSON FOR SUBMISSION

1. Explain the notion of communicative competence.
2. How would you characterize the linguistic situation of Hispanic bilinguals in North America? What about that of the bilingual Basque-American community?
3. Why is it important to define degrees of bilingualism? How can you define the degree of bilingualism of a Basque-American bilingual? Imagine that you want to classify Basque-American bilinguals according to their proficiency in Basque and English. Establish some linguistic and social criteria for doing so.

16 · Basque-based pidgins

PIDGIN varieties have developed in language contact situations throughout the world when speakers of three or more different languages need common linguistic ground to communicate for certain limited purposes. The development of pidgin varieties, for example, was common among traders and in colonization situations. Here is a likely scenario: Some Europeans establish relations with speakers of another area, such as Africans or Native Americans, in order to trade with them. (In fact, the word *pidgin* is probably derived from the English word *business*.) Not speaking the same language, they develop a simplified, mixed variety for the purpose of the short communicative interactions in which they will be engaging. Pidgins are usually based on the language of the economically dominant people. They have no native speakers, and are used in very limited situations. These varieties are not simply the result of heavy borrowing or "bad X"; they are totally independent varieties.

Many pidgins were created by African slaves on plantations throughout America. Plantation owners put slaves of different tribes together so they could not communicate and rebel. Slaves developed pidgin languages taking lexicon from the European language of their oppressors, and mixing it with simplified grammatical characteristics of all the languages they spoke. In such situations, since communication was needed in a wider range of situations, and slaves belonging to different groups ended up marrying, their children acquired the pidgin as their native tongue and developed it further. The pidgin then became a creole. Some examples of creole varieties still used today are Jamaican Creole, Hawaiian Creole, and Tok Pisin.

Evidence of the presence of incipient Basque pidgins in the sixteenth and seventeenth centuries has been found. In the seventeenth century, an Icelandic Basque pidgin arose from the interaction between Basque fishermen and Icelandic natives, as shown by both historical and linguistic data. This variety contains mostly Basque lexicon, but the structure is not Basque.

Differing from Basque, Icelandic Basque pidgin morphology is unmarked: Nouns are unmarked for case, and verbs have a unique form not marked for aspect or tense and without agreement features (Hualde, 1991b). For instance:

Example 16.1
Christ Maria presenta for mi balia,
'If Christ and Mary give me a whale',

for mi, presenta for ju bustana
'I will give you the tail'

In example 16.1, lexical items such as *balia* 'whale' and *bustana* 'tail' are without doubt Basque. In addition, the subject of the first sentence carries no case marking (Basque: *Christ Maria-k*) and the two verbs show a unique form with no morphological marking: *presenta* 'if they give me' (Basque: *ematen badidate*) and 'I will give you' (Basque: *emango dizut*).

IN ADDITION, word order is fixed (S-V-IO-DO), following the Icelandic model, as we can see in example 16.1. The presence of Basque determiner -*a*, reinterpreted as part of the noun or adjective, is also a common characteristic of Basque pidgins.

Basque pidgin

Pidgins are reduced varieties created in language contact situations by speakers of different languages. When in the seventeenth century, Basque fishermen needed to trade with Icelandic natives, they together developed a Basque pidgin.

BAKKER (1989) provides mostly historical data to show Basque–American Indian pidgin varieties used in the sixteenth and seventeenth centuries along the Canadian eastern coast. In the few surviving documents, Bakker found Basque words such as *adesquidé* 'friend' (today *adiskide* in Basque) and *ania* 'brother' (today *anaia*).

IMPORTANT CONCEPTS
Pidgin: A reduced language that results from extended language contact between groups of people with no language in common, often for business purposes. Unnecessary grammatical complications are reduced to make communication easier.

Creole: When a pidgin variety is learned natively by the children of the community, it is considered a *creole*. In the process of nativization, the opposite of a pidginization process happens: The grammar, phonology and lexicon of this variety are further developed.

Substrate language: The language of the less powerful group. This group accommodates more and takes the lexicon of the more powerful group.

Superstrate language: Usually the language of the more powerful group. This language provides most of the lexicon.

Lesson sixteen

LEARNING OBJECTIVES

1. Define and be able to describe the main characteristics of a pidgin variety.
2. Consider the linguistic and social aspects of pidgin varieties.
3. Assess historical and linguistic evidence of the existence of incipient pidgin varieties based on Basque as the substrate language.

REQUIRED READING

Bakker, P. 1989. " 'The Language of the Coast Tribes is Half Basque': A Basque-American Indian Pidgin, 1540–1640," *Anthropological Linguistics* 31(3–4): 117–48.

Hualde, J. I. 1991b. "Icelandic Basque Pidgin," *Anuario del Seminario de Filología Vasca Julio de Urquijo* 25(2): 427–37.

SUGGESTED READING
Hualde, J. I. 1988. "Euskararen ume ezezaguna: Euskal Herriko bale arrantzaleen truke-hizkuntza." *Jakin*, vol. 48: 53–62.

WRITTEN LESSON FOR SUBMISSION
1. Why did Basque pidgins not develop into creole languages?
2. Purists often compare contact varieties with heavy borrowing, such as certain kinds of Basque in contact with Spanish or Spanish in contact with English, with pidgin varieties. Is the Spanish with heavy transfer from English used by Hispanics in New York or the Southwest (Spanglish), or the Basque used with heavy transfer from Spanish, English, or French comparable to pidgin varieties? Describe the similarities and differences between pidgins and the varieties just listed.

17 · Ethnicity Maintenance
The American West

T HE FIRST Basque presence in North America dates
from the 1850s. Harsh economic conditions in
Europe combined with the Basque tradition of inheritance (whereby one sibling inherited the whole household) led many Basques to emigrate. The great majority
came from rural areas and ended up working in the
American sheep industry. Successful immigrants
encouraged relatives and hometown friends to follow
them to the New World, which provoked important
chain migration. Uninterrupted immigration established links for decades with the Old World and helped
keep Basque ethnicity intact. Beginning in the 1960s,
better economic, political, and social conditions in
Europe resulted in a steep decline in Basque emigration.
Currently, few Basques in the United States earn their
living from the sheep industry, and most are fully integrated into American society.

Since Basques were never officially recognized as
belonging to a unique political entity, they were not
recorded as such. It is, therefore, difficult to estimate the
number living in the diaspora. In any case, if we invoke
Basqueness as a concept, a definition is required. Differing from current tendencies in the Basque Country (see
Chapter 8), but in line with those of early Basque nationalism (see Chapter 22) and American immigrant communities, Basques in North America currently define
their ethnicity in biological terms: People of Basque
ancestry are considered Basque by the community
regardless of whether they speak Basque or not, whether
they are active members in the Basque-American community, or whether they participate in Basque cultural
activities, and regardless of which American-born gener-

ation they belong to. In essence, we can say that, as the Basque community integrated into American society, typical ethnic markers, such as the language, lost importance in a definition of Basque identity.

F ROM A historical perspective, Basque hotels can be considered the first Basque ethnic marker in the American West. Hotels served as microcosms of the Basque Country. In the hotels, immigrants could spend their vacations, rest when they were sick (women even went to Basque hotels to deliver their babies and recover under the care of the hotel wife, who was also usually Basque), and spend their free time living exactly as they had at home.

The first generation most often did not integrate into American society, and many returned home after a few years of hard work. Most of those who stayed married fellow Basques, and little by little they became more integrated into the host society.

Second generation Basque-Americans often grew up surrounded by Basque speakers in an environment highly charged with Basque values and symbols. They worked in different fields, however, and they became better integrated into American society. For the second generation, a sense of Basque ethnic identity was no longer linked to a rural (*baserri-giroa* 'rural work-related') context, and instead came to be associated with leisure activity. During the 1960s, Basque clubs were founded to concentrate efforts on cultural and recreational displays of Basque ethnicity. Basques involved in these clubs started to hold annual picnics and festivals, and to establish Basque dance groups and choirs.

With respect to language, as with other ethnic groups in North America, the maintenance of the immigrant language is not an absolute condition in ethnic conceptions. Use of English becomes necessary for social

Ongi Etorri Danaki

JAIALDI 2000
INTERNATIONAL
BASQUE CULTURAL FESTIVAL

JULY 27 · 28 · 29 · 30
BOISE, IDAHO

Jaialdi: showing Basqueness in Boise
This poster announces Jaialdi, a massive Basque festival
held every five years in Boise, Idaho. Since language
maintenance is not an absolute condition to claim
Basque ethnicity, other markers are used instead, such
as folklore, cuisine or display of flags.

mobility, and the ethnic language loses importance in a definition of ethnicity. At the time when Douglass and Bilbao conducted their study (1975), Basque was widely used among immigrants; first-generation Americans had some knowledge of Basque, but this eroded rapidly. Language retention among those born in America was correlated with parent occupation and sibling age order. When parents were engaged in the sheep industry or worked at a Basque hotel, children retained Basque. In addition, older children usually learned more Basque than did younger ones. Douglass and Bilbao also mention that second-generation Basque-Americans rarely learned any Basque.

AT PRESENT, since the Basque community is more integrated into American society than ever before, and immigration from the Basque Country has essentially ceased, Basque language retention is more problematic than ever. However, an increasing number of Basque-Americans take Basque language lessons and even go to the Basque Country to learn the language of their ancestors.

Lesson seventeen

LEARNING OBJECTIVES
1. Appreciate the relationship between language loyalty and ethnicity maintenance.
2. Identify Basque ethnic markers in the American West.
3. Explore the role that language plays in a definition of Basque identity in the American West.

REQUIRED READING

Douglass, W. A., and J. Bilbao. 1975. "Ethnicity Mainte-
nance among Basque-Americans" in *Amerikanuak:
Basques in the New World*, 327–96. Reno: Univ. of
Nevada Press.

SUGGESTED READING

Fernández de Larrinoa, K. 1992. *Estatu Batuetako
mendebalde urrutiko euskal jaiak.* Vitoria-Gasteiz:
Basque Government Press.

WRITTEN LESSON FOR SUBMISSION

1. According to Fernández de Larrinoa, "Basqueness is
   not an absolute category; on the contrary, it arose
   and continues to exist as the result of specific social
   and cultural practices. Basqueness is a cultural category that is neither static nor homogeneous, but has
   changed through time" (1992: 22).Comment on Fernández de Larrinoa's definition of Basqueness.
2. Briefly explain the ethnic markers given by Douglass
   and Bilbao (1975) for the Basque-American community and compare them to current ones in North or
   South America.

18 · **Language Maintenance and Change**
American Basque

THE BASQUE-SPEAKING community in Elko, Nevada, provides a good locus of study for anybody interested in language-contact and dialect-contact situations. Since Basque is in contact with English in Elko, linguistic change observed in the Basque Country and often attributed to the external influence of Spanish or French can be compared with similar linguistic processes occurring in the Basque of Elko. The comparison of European and American Basque can shed light on issues such as external influence and universal tendencies in linguistic change. In addition, since speakers of different Basque dialects interact in Elko, examination of this variety may underline intralanguage accommodation processes among speakers of different Basque regional dialects.

Even though the Elko Basque-speaking community has been rather important, the current situation of Basque provides no reason for optimism about its future. Basque is not being transmitted within the family, except in a few cases, and there is no significant immigration of European Basque speakers to keep the language alive. Since the Basques in Elko are decreasing in numbers, and Basque speakers have tended to marry non-Basque speakers, the number of Basque-speaking social networks and the possibility of using the minority language have been radically reduced.

IMPORTANT CONCEPTS
Several linguistic characteristics are common to the Basque spoken in Elko.

Reduced Basque and *Full Basque: Reduced Basque* (RB) refers here to Basque as spoken in the diaspora, in this case in Elko. It is opposed to *Full Basque* (FB)—the Basque spoken by fully competent natives in the Basque Country. As noted in Amorrortu (1995, 2000b), these terms are relative. There is no doubt that bilingual speakers may not be fully competent Basque speakers in the Basque Country either, especially given that Basque is a minority language there as well, and its use is also restricted. Away from their native community, speakers in the diaspora usually have even fewer opportunities to use their native language, and linguistic changes are to be expected.

Emigré Basque and *American Basque*: *Emigré Basque* (EB) refers to Basque spoken by immigrants. Basque is a native (first) language, although many immigrants may now use English more. *American Basque* (AB) is the variety used by those born in America who learned Basque natively. American Basques usually use their native language in very reduced circumstances.

First language and *second languages*: the terms first and second refer to order of acquisition. A *first language* is a native language; a second language is a language learned after acquiring a first language. *Second languages* are often learned by instruction.

Primary language and *secondary languages*: These terms refer to the use speakers make of their languages. A *primary language* is the one used most in an individual's everyday life; a *secondary language* is one used in a fewer number of contexts. In immigrant situations, Basque is usually the first language, but it is most often secondary.

Attrition phenomena: *Attrition* or language loss phenomena are usually found in contact situations, but especially diaspora cases. Since immigrants lack the

Interdialectal forms

Oral interaction among speakers of different dialects in the American West has induced brought about the creation of interdialectal forms.

Photo from Douglass and Bilbao (1975)

---

opportunity to use their native language in a wide variety of situations, and live away from the prescriptivist pressure of the native community, it is easy to find linguistic change. Reduced language use makes speakers lose morphological distinctions, often overgeneralizing the use of simpler (18.1) or unmarked (18.3) structures instead of others that are cognitively more complex to process (18.2 and 18.4, respectively). For instance:

Example 18.1
RB: *egiten ahal dut*   'I can do it'

Example 18.2
FB: Western: *egin neike*   'I can do it'
    Central: *egin dezaket*   'I can do it'

Example 18.3

AB: *karniseroa*	*eman*	*du*	*aragia*	*kozineroak*
butcher:	give	AUX:	meat:	cooks:
abs		obj	abs	abs

'the butcher gave meat to the chefs'

Example 18.4

FB: *karnizeroak*	*eman*	*die*	*haragia*	*kozineroei*
butcher:	give	AUX:	meat:	cooks:
erg		obj, dat	abs	dat

'the butcher gave meat to the chefs'

EXAMPLE 18.1 illustrates the use of particle *ahal* to make the potential with an indicative auxiliary verb, instead of the appropriate potential specific auxiliary shown in example 18.2. Example 18.3 shows neutralization of ergative and dative declension cases, using the absolutive instead, and loss of case concordance in the auxiliary verb.

Accommodation phenomena: Nevada Basques come from differing linguistic backgrounds. Most speakers in Elko are from the Bizkaian coast, although some are from Navarre. Oral interaction among speakers of different dialects has brought about the creation of interdialectal forms—forms present in neither dialect. Forms such as example 18.5 contain a Navarrese demonstrative adjective form and anteposition of the demonstrative, which is characteristic of Bizkaian. Such forms were used by both Bizkaian and Navarrese speakers.

Example 18.5

EB:	*ek*	*euskaldunak*
	these: abs	Basques: abs

'these Basque speakers'

Example 18.6
FB: Navarrese: *euskaldun*   *hek*
                       Basque   these: abs
        Bizkaian: *honeek*   *euskaldunak*
                       these: abs   Basques: abs
        'these Basque speakers'

English influence: The influence of English is most clearly observed at the lexical level. Loanwords such as *estorra* 'store', *troka* 'truck', *aiskrimia* 'ice cream', and *postofiza* 'post office' are commonly used among Basque speakers in the United States.

Acceleration of a change already produced in the Basque Country: Other linguistic phenomena began in Europe and accelerated in the diaspora. For example, the use of anteposed demonstrative adjectives in the absolutive (18.7) or genitive (18.8) with the noun inflected in the corresponding case:

Example 18.7
EB: *orrek*   *etxietan*
        those: abs   houses: ines
        'in those houses'

FB: Bizkaian: *horreetan*   *etxeetan*
                        those: ines   houses: ines
                        'in those houses'

Example 18.8
EB: *orren*   *terrenoetara*
        these: gen   fields: all
        'to these fields'

FB: Bizkaian: *horreetara*   *terrenoetara*
                        these: all   fields: all

THIS CHANGE has been documented for Full Lekeitian Basque (Hualde et al., 1994). Therefore, it cannot be explained as attrition phenomenon. In addition, it does not involve any simplification. Finally, since there is no parallel structure in either English or Spanish, we can discard the external-influence hypothesis.

Lesson eighteen

LEARNING OBJECTIVES
1. Consider linguistic accommodation as a possible origin of language change in a multidialectal situation.
2. Compare internally and externally induced language change.
3. Evaluate language attrition and language transfer phenomena.
4. Distinguish first and primary languages, on the one hand, and second and secondary languages, on the other.

REQUIRED READING
Amorrortu, E. 2000b. "Is American Basque a Unified Variety? Structural Changes in the Basque of Elko, Nevada," *Journal of Basque Studies*, vol. 20: 105–18.
———. 1995. "Retention and Accommodation in the Basque of Elko, Nevada," *Anuario de Filología Vasca Julio de Urquijo*, vol. 29, no. 2: 407–29. Donostia: Gipuzkoako Foru Aldundia.

SUGGESTED READING
Silva-Corvalán, C. 1994. *Language Contact and Change: Spanish in Los Angeles*. Oxford: Clarendon Press.

WRITTEN LESSON FOR SUBMISSION

1. Puristic views of language associate linguistic change with corruption. Do you think linguistic change is negative? Are older linguistic forms inherently better than newer ones? Do you consider change in any aspect of life something to avoid?

2. Explain transfer at the lexical level, and give some examples of lexical items borrowed by English from another language. To which semantic fields do the borrowings you gave belong? Do you think English speakers could or should manage without borrowing those words? Why or why not?

3. If you belong to the Basque-American community, can you give any examples of Basque borrowings into English, or English borrowings into Basque?

19 · **Bertsolaritza**

BASQUE improvised singing, *Bertsolaritza*, is an important oral cultural tradition which draws thousands of people for national contests. An oral poet or troubadour (*bertsolari*) spontaneously composes and sings verses "online" following traditional guidelines and rules. Bertsolaritza is considered the most important display of Basque traditional oral literature. Its inclusion in a sociolinguistics textbook is justified for two reasons: First, it is a cultural manifestation where use and mastery of language are essential; and second, it became an important social movement with implications for the reversal language shift movement.

Not only is Basque the only language used in bertsolaritza, but modern use of Basque and dialectal and register variation are necessary for the successful bertsolari. In addition, bertsolaritza serves as a dialectics exercise where bertsolaries need to pay as much attention to form as to content. On the one hand, they are quite constrained by the formal rules; on the other, they have to come up quickly with ideas, link them appropriately, and make them accessible to the audience in an original way.

MAIN CHARACTERISTICS OF BERTSOLARITZA
Popular activity: Representation of popular culture. Although current bertsolaries are most often highly educated, traditional ones used to be illiterate. Fans who follow the activity today include both the schooled and the unschooled.

Improvisation: There is no time to prepare, edit, or organize. Bertsolaritza requires of the poet the ability to fully master the language, to come up with ideas quickly, organize them, and put them into words. In addition, the bertsolari needs to have a good memory to remember rhymes as well as good concentration to come up with the *bertso* 'stanza'.

Atzekoz aurrera 'backwards technique': The climax is always placed at the end of the turn. The bertsolari thinks about the end first, and then organizes the whole turn to direct it toward the ending "punch."

Since it is oral and improvised, bertsolaritza requires *fast production* and fast movement of images and ideas.

Before describing the formal characteristics of bertsolaritza, let's examine a bertso 'stanza' composed by Jon Lopategi:

Urepel hortan bazen artzain bat
*izarrekin mintzo **zena***
agian, holan sortu zitzaion
*bertsoetarako **sena**,*
sentimendutan sakon bezain
*arrazoiketan **zuzena***
Xalbador deitzen zioten baina
*Fernando zuen **izena***

There was a shepherd in Urepel
who talked to the stars
maybe, that way,
his good sense for bertsos developed
he was as deep in feelings
as correct in reasoning
people called him Xalbador
but his name was Fernando

THIS BERTSO is made up of eight *bertsolerros* or 'lines', four of which rhyme: the second (*zena*), fourth (*sena*), sixth (*zuzena*), and eighth (*izena*). This kind of bertso is called *zortziko handia* 'eight-verse major' because it contains eight verses: Odd verses have ten syllables, and even ones have eight. Table 19-1 shows the most often used metric patterns in Basque oral tradition.

Table 19-1
Most Popular Metric Patterns in Bertsolaritza

Hamarreko Nagusia Ten-verse Major	Zortziko Nagusia Eight-verse Major	Hamarreko Txikia Ten-verse Minor	Zortziko Txikia Eight-verse Minor stanza	Bederatzi Puntukoa Nine rhymed verse-
10-	10-	7-	7-	7-
8A	8A	6A	6A	6A
10-	10-	7-	7-	7-
8A	8A	6A	6A	5A
10-	10-	7-	7-	7-
8A	8A	6A	6A	6A
10-	10-	7-	7-	7-
8A	8A	6A	6A	6A
10-		7-		6A
8A		6A		6A
				6A
				6A
				7-
				5A

Women bertsolaries
In contrast to the tradition, the urban, the highly-educated, and women are now actively participating in bertsolaritza. Maialen Lujambio, shown in this photo, won the second position in the 2001 national contest.
Photo from Euskal Etxeak 53:16.

Hamarreko nagusia 'ten-verse major', for example, contains ten verses; all even verses contain eight syllables and the same rhyme, and odd verses contain ten syllables and do not rhyme. Probably the most difficult to compose, *bederatzi puntukoa* is made up of fourteen verses and nine rhymes in exactly the pattern indicated in Table 19-1.

THE BERTSOLARI tries to make consonantal rhymes using verse-final words that rhyme in both vowels and consonants (like the rhyme given in the Lopategi's bertso quoted above). Vocalic rhymes and rhymes made by adding a suffix, for example, are considered poor ones. *Poto*, using the same word for rhyming, is highly penalized, unless the word is used with different meanings.

THERE ARE different types of exercises in bertsolaritza: Bertsolaries may sing in pairs, taking turns after a bertso is finished to answer each other while each plays a different role; or they may co-construct a bertso, composing a verse each until the bertso is finished. They may also sing alone, after being given four rhymed words, or a first or final rhymed verse, or a topic. The people responsible for selecting and giving the topics (*gai-jartzaileak*) are continually coming up with new ideas for different types of exercises.

The main activities a bertsolari may be involved in are the following:

1. Informal exercise among friends whose only object is entertainment.
2. Desafio or 'challenge' exercise: Challenge between two or more bertsolaries to prove who is better.
3. Lore-jokoak or 'floral games': Contests during festivals or celebrations, most often as written exercises.
4. Txapelketak: Contests to prove who is the best. The winner gets a txapela 'beret'. All participants sing under the same circumstances. National contests are becoming extremely popular. Thousands of people come from all over the Basque Country to attend the competition, which lasts for weeks, and the final event is broadcast live by ETB and several radio stations.

To conclude, bertsolaritza is a popular activity that closely reflects the concerns of Basque society. Political issues, recent events, expression of different feelings, and declarations supporting Euskara are common topics used in performances. During the last few decades, bertsolaritza has also reflected many of the social changes that have occurred in Basque society: It went from being linked mainly to rural society to being more common in urban contexts; in contrast to the prior male-only tradition, many young women are now participating at the highest level; and today most young bertsolaries are highly educated and received formal instruction in *bertso-eskolas,* schools created with the only objective of training bertsolaries. The types of exercises are also changing, becoming more innovative and combining the bertsolaritza activity with music, theater, and other popular cultural manifestations.

Lesson nineteen

LEARNING OBJECTIVES

1. Recognize the importance of bertsolaritza as a social movement and in its connection to the language recovery movement.
2. Identify the formal characteristics of bertsolaritza.
3. Explore the improvisation technique that characterizes bertsolaritza.
4. Understand the "backwards technique."
5. Become acquainted with poto.
6. Learn about different types of exercises for bertsolaritza.

REQUIRED READING

Aulestia, G. 1995. *Improvisational Poetry from the Basque Country,* 16–46, 57–62. Reno: Univ. of Nevada Press.

Zulaika, J. 1988. "The Bertsolariak," in *Basque Violence: Metaphor and Sacrament,* 209–30. Reno: Univ. of Nevada Press.

SUGGESTED READING

Lekuona, J. M. 1982. *Ahozko Euskal Literatura*, chap. 6
(91–108) and chap. 9 (139–70). Donostia: Erein.

INTERNET RESOURCES

The Basque Government site for the Department of Culture provides a good explanation in English of what bertsolaritza is, how a bertso is composed, the history of bertsolaritza, kinds of exercises, training schools, and Bertsozale Elkartea (Association of Bertsolari Enthusiasts): http://www1.euskadi.net/kultura/literatura/bertso00_i.htm

Bertsolari, a journal on bertsolaritza (only available in Basque) that is published every three months by the Bertsozale Elkartea: http://www.bertsolari.net

WRITTEN LESSON FOR SUBMISSION

1. Try to write a bertso in English following the rules of Bertsolaritza: you can choose any metric and rhyme pattern. Remember not to do poto.
2. After you write your bertso, answer the following questions: Do you think it is easier or harder to write a poem in English than in Basque? Following the rules and guides of Bertsolaritza, is it as easy or hard to improvise a bertso in English as it is in Basque?
3. The bertsolari gives the punch of the turn at the end. Why? Do you think the "backwards technique" has anything to do with the left-branching (head-final) character of the Basque language? Why or why not?

20 · Forms of Address

THE STUDY of forms of address—the words used to refer to someone spoken or written to—in a given language is a topic of great interest for linguists, sociologists, and anthropologists. It is especially interesting from the point of view of linguistic variation, since forms of address show both situational and social appropriateness rules in a given linguistic community. For instance, English speakers use different titles to address doctors or professors, when appropriate. Basque speakers may also address high-status people using addressing formulae, such as:

Example 20.1
On Jose Miguel Barandiaran 'Mr. Barandiaran'

Example 20.2
Lehendakari Jauna 'Mr. President'

Or even more formal formulae in letters, such as:

Example 20.3
Andre txit agurgarria 'The Honorable (F)'

Apart from addressing formulae, Basque presents a complex system of addressing terms, which can be marked in the use of personal pronouns and verbal morphology. Table 19-1 shows Basque personal pronouns.

There are four second-person singular personal pronouns in Basque: a neutral *zu*, intimate *hi* and *xu*, and formal *berori*. Plural second-person pronouns are reduced to two forms: neutral and intimate *zuek* and extremely formal *berorrek*, which is an archaic form in most varieties.

Basque verbal morphology can also encode social relationships. There are three kinds of verbal forms in Basque:

1. Neutral forms do not show agreement with an allocutive second person:

   etorri   *naiz*
   come   AUX: 1sg
   'I came'

2. Other forms agree with an argumental second person:

   etorri   *haiz*
   come   AUX: 2sg
   'you came'

3. Finally, allocutive forms show agreement with an allocutive second person:

   etorri   *nauk*
   come   AUX: 1sg-allocM
   'I came (male addressee)'
   etorri   *naun*
   come   AUX: 1sg-allocF
   'I came (female addressee)'

Allocutive forms (20.4) are those in which the inflected verb agrees with the addressee in person and gender, and the latter is not an argument selected by the verb.

Example 20.4
gaur   goizean   etorri   *nauk/naun*
today   morning: ines come   AUX: 1sg-alloc: M/F
'I came this morning'

Probably the oldest treatment, *hika*, has the peculiarity of encoding the only old gender distinction in Basque.

The gender of the addressee, when singular, is encoded in the verbal form, although the corresponding pronoun (*hi* 'you sg') is invariable for gender. See example 20.5.

Example 20.5

baina	(hi)	ez	*haiz*	egon
but	(you)	neg	AUX: 2sg	be

'but you were not (there)'

IN EXAMPLE 20.4, the addressee is encoded in the verb even though it is not an argument of the sentence; this communicates something like "I came this morning; I am talking to you male/female." In example 20.5, the addressee is an argument of the sentence. In fact, the addressee is the subject of the sentence and, unlike in examples 20.6 and 20.7, s/he is treated in a more familiar or friendly way.

Example 20.6

gaur	goizean	etorri	*naiz*
today	morning: ines	come	AUX: 1sg

'I came this morning'

Example 20.7

baina	(zu)	ez	*zara*	egon
but	(you)	neg	AUX: 2sg	be

'but you were not (there)'

Once the formal side of allocutive forms has been explained, we need to address the social meaning of the different forms of address. Today, the most neutral form is *zuka*, and *hika* can be considered markedly familiar or intimate in most varieties. There is dialectal variation both in the forms and their use. Hika is used throughout the Basque Country, although not by all speakers:

Men use hika more than women and interior inhabitants use it more than coastal ones. In fact, the social rules that regulate the use of hika are not the same across regions.

Some varieties of Bizkaian still use the very respectful form *berorika*, which is conjugated in the third person (similar to Spanish *usted*). In addition, Eastern dialects have allocutive forms other than hika: *zuka* (neutral) and *xuka* (familiar, mostly used among and to address women). The situational use of all these treatments is rather complex and, as stated before, varies across regions.

USING A direct questionnaire throughout the Basque Country, Alberdi (1996) examined the situational use of hika (T, or familiar, versus *zuka* V, or formal; the use of the abbreviations T and V comes from the Latin *tu* and *vos*) and drew some general conclusions:

1. Hika is used asymmetrically within the family; in other words, although parents may address their children in hika (T), the latter address the former always in zuka (V). In addition, Basque social rules forgive the use of T among spouses and to younger children.

Table 19-1
Basque Second-Person Personal Pronouns

Pronouns	Treatment
zu	zuka
hi	hika: toka (M), noka (F)
xu	xuka
berori	berorika
zuek	zuka
berorrek	berorika

Forms of address

Several treatments are used within the family: parents may address their children in hika, whereas the latter address the former always in zuka. In addition, Basque social rules forgive the use of hika among spouses and to younger children.

---

2. The use of hika outside the family is marked. Speakers of the same sex and age have the highest possibility of using T, even when they are not close friends.

HISTORICAL linguists point to the antiquity of the hika system in Basque. Alberdi establishes the following stages in the development of forms of the address system:

1. The personal pronoun hi, which requires the use of allocutive forms, is the only second-person singular pronoun in the oldest stage.
2. Zu starts to be used as a singular form of respect.

3. Consequently, allocutive forms of zu are developed in eastern dialects by analogy with allocutive hika.
4. Forms like zure mesedeori 'your grace', zure senoria 'your lordship', and berori 'you: respectful-sg', all of which require third-person agreement, appeared during the sixteenth or seventeenth century.
5. Lastly, allocutive xuka appears more recently in Eastern dialects as a palatalization of zuka.

IMPORTANT CONCEPTS
Allocutivity: Agreement with an allocutive or ethnic second person when the second person is not an argument in the sentence, as shown in examples 20.8 and 20.9.

Example 20.8
Mikel	*diñat*	*izena*
Mikel: abs	V: 1sg-allocF	name: abs

'My name is Mikel'

Example 20.9
bazkaltzera	*etorri*	*gaituk*
eat lunch: all	come	AUX: 1pl-allocM

'We came to eat lunch'

The semantics of power and solidarity: There are two basic dimensions in social interaction (see also Chapter 9). On one hand, there is a hierarchical and nonreciprocal relationship between people occupying unequal power positions: The one holding more power (a boss, a parent, a teacher, an official) uses T and the one holding less power (an employee, a child, a student, a citizen) uses V. On the other, people in similar positions of power express their symmetrical relationship by using T to each other, along a solidarity dimension.

Lesson twenty

LEARNING OBJECTIVES
1. Appreciate the social meanings attached to Basque forms of address.
2. Examine linguistic practices in relation to gender.
3. Describe the formal basics of the hika system.
4. Learn about the social and situational use of hika.
5. Assess the historical development of forms of address.

REQUIRED READING

Alberdi, J. 1995. "The Development of the Basque System of Terms of Address and the Allocutive Conjugation," in J. I. Hualde, J. A. Lakarra, and R. L. Trask (eds.), *Towards a History of the Basque Language*, 275–93. Amsterdam/Philadephia: John Benjamins Publ.

Brown, R., and A. Gilman. 1960. "The Pronouns of Power and Solidarity," in T. A. Sebeok (ed.), *Style in Language*, 253–76. New York: Technology Press of MIT.

De Rijk, R. P. 1998. "Familiarity or Solidarity: The Pronoun Hi in Basque," in *De Lingua Vasconum*, 297–300. Bilbao: Univ. of the Basque Country.

SUGGESTED READING

Alberdi, J. 1996. *Euskararen tratamenduak, erabilera*, 19–39, 119–30. Bilbao: Royal Academy of the Basque Language.

WRITTEN LESSON FOR SUBMISSION
1. Taking Brown and Gilman's article (1960) into account, answer the following question: According to Basque linguists, the Basque pronoun zu was used in

the past as a second-person plural pronoun, and only later did it come to mean second-person singular formal. Compare this process to similar phenomena in other languages.

2. If there were once a universal use of hika and at some point in history variation in forms of address arose in Basque, does this indicate a desire for greater social differentiation at that point?

3. What do you make of the complexity of forms of address in Basque with respect to social relations? Can we draw social conclusions about how Basque society was and is structured from linguistic facts such as forms of address?

IN THIS chapter, we address ideology in gender-based language. By examining the social use of hika, we will learn about how language ideology affects the way different social groups use language in Basque society. As noted in the previous chapter, the situational and geographical use of hika varies to a great degree. A survey throughout the Basque Country (Alberdi, 1996) based on direct questioning showed overall gender, age, and geographical differences in the use of hika. Table 21-1 summarizes some of the quantitative differences in the use of *toka* (male-addressee form of hika) and *noka* (female -addressee form of hika) across situations of use:

Table 21-1:

Quantitative *toka* and *noka* use in situations of use

Toka			*Noka*
girlfriend			boyfriend
to boyfriend	33.50%	21.10%	to girlfriend
brother			sister
to brother	90.30%	49.40%	to sister
sister			brother
to brother	72.30%	50.20%	to sister
father			mother
to son	69.80%	30.30%	to daughter
mother			father
to son	63%	28.00%	to daughter

Adapted from Alberdi 1996:371

Not only do women use hika less than men, but women are also addressed less often in hika than men, even when both interlocutors are women.

In an ethnographic study of the male and female usage of and attitudes toward hika forms among Basque-educated secondary school students in the Donostia area, Echeverria (2000) claims that Basque language ideology recursively constructs a link between ethnic authenticity, masculinity, and particular linguistic forms—in this case, hika forms. An androcentric view of Basque society is perpetuated recursively in language ideology. Echeverria establishes the parallelisms laid out in Table 21-2.

Table 21-2
Recursiveness in language ideology

status / solidarity
Spanish / Basque
Batua / vernacular (herrikoa)
zuka / hika
artificiality / authenticity

Adapted from Echeverria, 2000

In Echeverria's view, the dichotomy between status and solidarity represented in how Spanish (the prestigious variety) and Basque (the variety favored in the solidarity dimension) were perceived by the students is projected in the relationship between Batua (prestigious) and vernacular (solidarity), as well as in that between zuka (prestigious) and hika (solidarity).

THE USE of hika is associated with "the authentic," solidarity, and men's speech. Hika seems to carry the social meaning of authenticity because it is used in Basque cultural activities considered authentic (like

Men's and women's speech
Women generally use Hika less than men, maybe
because they show greater concern for politeness and
social relations.
By permission of DEIA.

---

pilota 'a Basque game or sport', or bertsolaritza). Since
those activities are mostly performed by men, people
associate men's linguistic practices (hika) with authentic Basque ethnicity, due to an iconic relationship
between hika and masculinity.

ACCORDING to Echeverria, the historical reason that
hika came to be associated with male speech may
be the result of the differing occupational roles of
women and men after urbanization. Men took jobs in
factories, while women were hired as maids, making it
necessary for them to show greater concern for politeness and social relations. This explanation implies that
the recession in hika use started among women living
in urban areas who, willing to distance themselves from

the social stigma of Basque on one hand, and language used by workers (rude speech, hika) on the other, turned to Spanish and zuka, respectively.

This explanation essentially coincides with the traditional sociolinguistic explanation of why prestigious forms are considered as such, and why stigmatized forms or varieties are not abandoned: Stigmatized forms are usually used by men and, according to the variationist literature, are stigmatized because they are associated with a hard, working-class lifestyle. Since women are supposedly more attuned to social concerns such as prestige, they abandon forms associated with social stigma. At the same time, these forms are also associated with covert prestige. In other words, they may be in-group identity markers, which would explain why men do not abandon them.

However, we must not forget that Romance languages have T/V addressing distinctions and that their societies had stronger social differences. Remember that the Basque bourgeoisie and nobility often turned to Spanish models as well. These external pressures may have influenced the spread of zuka forms, due to identification with higher sophistication and polite society in contact areas. In this context, Basque women working as maids for high-class Spanish-speaking or bilingual families may have abandoned the use of hika faster because they identified it with a *baserri* 'farm' lifestyle and a lack of sophistication.

In any case, the development of forms of address in Basque is very interesting since, in contrast to Indo-European languages (in which the use of more respectful forms is declining), hika, the more intimate form, is currently undergoing a process of historical, geographical, social, and situational reduction. This change appears to be due to the complexity of the hika system

_____

and the fact that, whereas all Basque speakers use the zuka system, only some also master the hika one. Language economy laws promote simplification in the direction of the system shared by all speakers.

_____

Lesson twenty-one

LEARNING OBJECTIVES
1. Identify gender patterns of Basque language use.
2. Pay attention to androcentricism in Basque traditional culture and secondary school textbooks.
3. Recognize language ideology as expressed in language use.

REQUIRED READING
Echeverria, B. 2000. *The Gendering of Basque Ethnic Identity*, chap. 4. UMI: Univ. of California, San Diego.

SUGGESTED READING
Alberdi, J. 1996. *Euskararen Tratamenduak: Erabilera*, 369–92, 417–22. Bilbao: Euskaltzaindia.

WRITTEN LESSON FOR SUBMISSION
1. Name three gender differences between male and female speech at any level of language in any language you know. Explain the phenomena and give detailed examples.
2. Why are there gender differences in the given language?
3. Do you think those differences are likely to increase or decrease in the given society? Why or why not?

MANY SITUATIONS demonstrate strong links between nationalist feelings and language. Sometimes, emphasis on a common language, despite other cultural differences, has led politicians to call for collective national identity common to different groups; in other situations, emphasis on a unique language, culture, and history has led nationalists to emphasize distinctiveness with respect to nearby groups. In any case, language plays an essential role in the creation and development of national identities. In this chapter, we explore the role that the Basque language played in nationalist conceptions at the beginning of Basque nationalism in the late nineteenth century and during the reversal language shift movement from the 1960s to today, the beginning of the twenty-first century.

The importance of Euskara in the development of Basque national identity has differed across time and has increased since a Basque nationalist ideology was born in the late nineteenth century, when the Basque bourgeoisie started to feel threatened by the increasing presence of Spanish immigrants attracted by the new employment opportunities in the industrial area of Western Bizkaia.

Euskara had already undergone severe language shift and was lost in most of Araba, Western Bizkaia, and the larger urban centers. The Basque urban bourgeoisie was, to a great degree, Spanish monolingual. Given this situation, it is not surprising that Basque nationalism's founder, Sabino Arana, did not attribute an important role to the Basque language in his new political conception. Rather than using linguistic or territorial criteria to define Basqueness, the genesis of Basque nationalist identity relied on racial arguments: Basques were those whose families were Basque for generations.

Given the conception of Basqueness based on race or ancestry, linguistic **purism** served as evidence of the purity of the Basque ethnic group: Arana's greatest linguistic concern was to keep Euskara free of loanwords. However, in contrast to the nineteenth-century "one nation, one language" idea, standardization and unification were not perceived as necessary. In fact, Arana promoted the use of different regional literary dialects, arguing that dialectal variation did not cause mutual intelligibility problems and, therefore, linguistic unification was unnecessary.

IN CONTRAST, modern Basque nationalism stresses the role of language in national self-conception. In the 1960s, at the end of the Franco dictatorship, Euskara became the key element in a definition of Basque identity and distinctiveness. According to Tejerina (1992, 1996), Basque awareness of language shift led Basque nationalists to accord the language a crucial symbolic role. The realization that their ancestral language was in the process of disappearing led Basque nationalists to redefine national consciousness and place cultural and, especially, linguistic recovery at the very center of their political project.

The rearticulation of Basque nationalism made the beginning of serious reversing language shift planning possible. As Euskara became seen as essential to Basque collective identity, Basque speakers started to shed themselves of the stigmatization previously associated with the use of Basque, and Spanish-monolingual speakers started to learn the language out of a desire to become integrated into the Basque-speaking community.

Beginning of nationalism
Sabino Arana, shown in this picture, did not attribute
an important role to the Basque language when consid-
ering Basque identity.

As already discussed in Chapter 7, when we
addressed corpus planning, Krutwig was primarily
responsible for the intellectual articulation of the role
that the Basque language plays in national identity; he
underlined the need for a single unified variety, along

with the idea that one nation needs one language —in the Basque case, *one strong variety*. With the increasing differentiation between radical nationalism and traditional nationalism in the 1980s, the former stressed the need for a unified variety of Basque, while the latter often promoted regional dialects. Recently, the differences have narrowed between radical and moderate nationalists with respect to the debate over regional dialects versus Batua. At the same time, displays of dialectal pride have increased everywhere, but especially in Bizkaian-speaking areas.

Basque nationalism in Iparralde is a much more recent phenomenon. Although for Basque nationalists—a minority of the population—the Basque language is an essential element of Basque identity, French nationalists do not normally stress Basque distinctiveness, and do not feel great attachment to their first language, favoring the majority national language of French. In fact, the Basque language is undergoing a severe shift process among the younger generations as already reported in Chapter 8. On the other hand, most Basque speakers there have not followed the linguistic unification movement promoted in the South, and the influence of Batua in the northern varieties is smaller.

COMING back to the idea that language plays an important role in all kinds of nationalism, it must be stressed that today both the Spanish and Basque languages are emphasized by Spanish and Basque nationalists as important defining traits of Spanish Constitutionalist and Basque distinctive identities respectively, which shows the importance that language continues to have on national conceptions.

POINTS OF INTEREST

1. Late nineteenth century: Arana formulates Basque nationalism. Basque identity is based on race. Linguistic purity is seen as proving the purity of the Basque race.

2. 1920s: Rise of linguistic consciousness; creation of first *ikastolas*. The Basque Studies Society starts the process of linguistic unification.

3. 1950s: Formation of Euzkadi Ta Askatasuna (ETA) 'Basque Homeland and Freedom'. Influenced by the Sapir-Whorfian hypothesis, ETA's founders consider survival of Basque crucial for maintaining Basque distinctiveness.

4. 1960s: Beginning of serious reversal language shift planning. Creation of AEK, a cooperative-based organization dedicated to Basque L2 teaching using communicative methodology. AEK established as its goals the spread of Batua and the rise of nationalist consciousness.

5. 1981: Creation of HABE, institutional effort to direct the L2 teaching movement. Association of AEK with radical, leftist nationalism, and HABE with moderate center-right nationalism. Intense political confrontation between the two organizations.

6. Late 1990s: Better relationship between AEK and HABE. Less identification between linguistic unification and radical nationalism. Increase in dialectal pride.

Lesson twenty-two

LEARNING OBJECTIVES

1. Trace the evolution in the importance gained by Euskara in Basque nationalism.
2. Explore the symbolic values of language in the construction of Basque modern national identity.
3. Situate linguistic purism in the context of nationalism.

REQUIRED READING

MacClancy, J. 1996. "Bilingualism and Multinationalism in the Basque Country," in C. Mar-Molinero and A. Smith (eds.), *Nationalism and the Nation in the Iberian Peninsula: Competing and Conflicting Identities*, 207–20. Berg: Oxford.

Tejerina, B. 1996. "Language and Basque Nationalism: Collective Identity, Social Conflict and Institutionalisation," in Mar-Molinero and Smith (eds.), *Nationalism and the Nation in the Iberian Peninsula. Competing and Conflicting Identities*, 221–36. Berg: Oxford.

SUGGESTED READING

Jausoro, M. N. 1996. *La práctica discursiva y el interdiscurso: Una propuesta metodológica para la investigación social del euskera*, 195–245. Leioa: Universidad del País Vasco.

Tejerina, B. 1992. *Lengua y Nación*, 138–344. Madrid: Siglo XXI.

WRITTEN LESSON FOR SUBMISSION

1. Evaluate the importance of language as a marker of collective American identity. Is English as important as Basque is in a conception of national identity?

Why? Does the diglossic situation of Basque have consequences for the creation of Basque national identity? Why?

2. Explain linguistic purity. Why do speakers of some languages, let's say French, for instance, favor the use of neologisms instead of direct borrowings of new lexical items?

23 · Ethnolinguistic Vitality, Social Identity

T HE THEORETICAL construct most often used to explain the interrelationships among language, ethnicity, and intergroup relations is *ethnolinguistic vitality*. Social psychologists have presented vitality as a predictor of all kinds of ethnolinguistic behavior, including language attitudes, language maintenance and loss, and bilingualism.

The social psychological approach to language in social interaction takes factors such as vitality and linguistic accommodation into account to explain individual speech behavior. The concept of ethnolinguistic vitality was first introduced by Giles, Bourhis, and Taylor (1977), and created as a tool for analyzing the sociostructural variables affecting the strength of ethnolinguistic communities within intergroup settings. The main objective of the construct is to predict linguistic behavior of members of those linguistic communities. In fact, the vitality of an ethnolinguistic group is defined as "that which makes a group likely to *behave* as a distinctive and collective entity within the intergroup setting" (Giles et al., 1977: 308, italics added). It is believed that groups with high vitality perceive in-group speakers. positively, whereas groups with low vitality perceive the out-group more favorably.

Ethnolinguistic vitality theory (ELV) is influenced by Tajfel's *social identity theory* and Giles' *speech accommodation theory*. According to *social identity theory*, identity is the result of an individual's evaluative ties to a particular group. Identity is a derivation of a person's social associations. Social identity is important for two reasons: First, social identity influences self-perception;

second, social associations are the more relevant behavioral markers.

Speech accommodation theory is concerned with the underlying motivations and social consequences of changes in speech styles. People are constantly modifying their speech to reduce (by converging) or accentuate (by diverging) the social and linguistic differences between them and their audience. The theory of accommodation is based on psychological research on similarity-attraction and the desire of a speaker for social approval. Psychologists suggest that a speaker can gain greater acceptance by reducing the dissimilarities with the interlocutor. Linguistic accommodation is seen as the speaker's attempt to modify her/his persona in order to make it more acceptable by accommodating to the interlocutor's speech. In converging, the speaker shows a favorable attitude toward the audience. In contrast, an individual may wish to distinguish her/himself from the addressee by diverging from the speech of the latter.

IN ACCORDANCE with social identity theory and speech accommodation theory, advocates of ELV theory predict that, in intergroup-conflict or diglossic situations, speakers from groups with high vitality will be less likely to converge with the out-group's speech than will those with low vitality. As a result of intergroup conflict situations, speakers are rewarded or sanctioned evaluatively, depending on the speech strategy (presence or absence of convergence) they use in intergroup encounters.

OBJECTIVE VITALITY

Three kinds of variables affect the *objective vitality* of speakers of a variety: status, demographic factors, and institutional factors. A speech community's vitality

Belonging to the group
Social identity can be explained as a derivation of a person's social associations. It influences self-perception and determines behavior, especially among youngsters.
Photo from Euskal Etxeak 36:15.

---

depends on the community's social status relative to other groups, both in the region and internationally. The group's status depends on its social prestige, its sociohistorical status, and the prestige of its language and culture. The more status a linguistic community has, the higher its vitality as a group. The status variables present some problems of quantification, however, and can only be determined through extensive ethnographic descriptions.

THE DEMOGRAPHIC characteristics of the linguistic group also contribute to its vitality. The number and percentage of speakers of a group with respect to other linguistic groups can sometimes have an influence on the group's vitality. Demographic trends in migration, mixed marriages, and birthrates also affect the vitality of the different groups in multilingual societies.

Finally, institutional support is another crucial factor when describing the objective ethnolinguistic vitality of a linguistic community. Institutional support is reflected in the particular variety's use in mass media, education, government services, industry, religion, culture, and politics. Ethnolinguistic groups who have positions of power in private and state institutions can increase their vitality as a collective entity, even as a demographic minority.

SUBJECTIVE VITALITY

IN A REVISION of the ethnolinguistic vitality theory, the concept of *subjective vitality* was introduced. The way group members *subjectively* perceive their vitality with respect to the vitality of other groups is viewed as a better predictor of linguistic behavior, because data on objective vitality do not always coincide with speakers' subjective views.

According to this theory, ethnolinguistic groups whose overall vitality is high will survive as collective entities, whereas groups with low vitality will lose their distinctiveness. However, promoters of this theory also acknowledge that sometimes perceptions of low vitality and threat of disappearance as a collective entity may give rise to a reaction by ethnolinguistic groups in support of their language and/or culture, thus potentially reversing the language-shift situation. This seems to have been the case at the beginning of the Basque recovery movement: A perception of Basque language and culture in serious danger of disappearing prompted a reaction by the Basque ethnolinguistic group to reverse the situation.

ELV AND THE BASQUE SITUATION

Attempts to apply the ELV theory to the Basque case lend credence to criticism that the theory has received. The application and quantification of the variables that form the vitality construct present difficulties. Demographic factors can be examined and determined quite accurately with the use of census and other demographic studies. Institutional factors are harder to evaluate, however, unless good descriptions of language use across situations are available to the researcher. Moreover, the status factors are related to a speech community's economic wealth, social status, and sociohistorical prestige, as well as the status of the language used by its speakers; they are thus hard to quantify, and subject to potentially flawed evaluation of historical materials. Because of this difficulty, this tool has often been used impressionistically. For example, one study of the effects of ethnolinguistic vitality and social identity on in-group bias and social attribution (Ros, Huici, and Cano, 1994), rated Basque status and institutional support in the BAC as having medium vitality without providing any objective data to support this rating.

A NOTHER study examined attitudes toward Spanish and Basque speakers among Basque-speaking university students, measuring the subjective vitality of the two languages with a questionnaire answered by the subjects under study (Amorrortu, 2000a). Tables 23-1 and 23-2 show Subjective Vitality ratings of Basque and Spanish, measured by seven indicators: perceived use in public administration, education, and mass media; perceived social prestige; number of speakers, future of the language; and perceived use in informal situations

Table 23-1
Subjective vitality of Basque

Basque vitality	Mean	Std. deviations
Administration	1.987	0.9217
Education	3.811	0.7119
Media	2.149	0.8987
Prestige	3.844	0.7765
Speakers	2.607	0.7208
Future	3.071	1.029
Street use	2.11	0.771

alpha=.705   mean=2.8

(street use). The five-point scale uses 1 for very low and 5 for very high.

Basque use in public administration (1.99), informal public settings (street use 2.11), and the media (2.15) is perceived as being rather low by respondents, when compared to the higher score given to prestige (3.84). Even though Basque prestige is perceived to be rather high, university Basque-speaking students perceive use of Basque and the number of speakers as being lower.

AS SHOWN in Table 23-2, Spanish vitality is perceived to be much higher than Basque vitality. As in the case of the subjective vitality of the Basque-speaking group, respondents also perceive the future of Spanish to differ from its present use: Respondents believe that the future prestige of the majority language is slightly lower (3.49) than is its current prestige (3.94), and remarkably lower than its current use in public informal life (use in the street is 4.20). These data may show an in-group bias of Basque speakers toward the minority language insofar as they anticipate a future for Basque

Table 23-2
Subjective vitality of Spanish

Spanish vitality	Mean	Std. deviations
Administration	4.147	0.8409
Education	1.993	0.9193
Media	4.032	0.8145
Prestige	3.943	0.8308
Speakers	3.541	0.9349
Future	3.493	1.084
Street use	4.198	0.7132

alpha=.66   mean=3.55

more positive than its present and, in a related way, a future in which Spanish use and prestige decline.

IN ANY case, the possible consequences of the subjective vitality of Basque and Spanish speakers needs to be taken with caution. Although the reported in-group bias and optimistic reaction of speakers of the minority language may be a good sign for Basque language maintenance, we need to remember that positive attitudes toward the language and good perceptions of the speakers do not guarantee language behavior. As discussed in Chapter 9, we need to distinguish between symbolic values assigned to Basque at a conscious level and subconscious perceptions of Basque speakers in status-related dimensions, and, especially, in solidarity-related dimensions. Despite conscious positive attitudes toward Basque and Basque speakers, unless language users subconsciously perceive Basque to be the language of intimate relationships, its use in informal and colloquial situations will not be guaranteed.

Linguistic Accommodation
Speakers modify their speech to reduce or accentuate
the social and linguistic differences between them and
their audience. Younger people, for instance, will gain
greater acceptance by reducing the dissimilarities with
peers.
Photo from Euskal Etxeak Especial 1999: 18

Lesson twenty-three

LEARNING OBJECTIVES
1. Understand the concept of ethnolinguistic vitality
   and its application to linguistic behavior.
2. Contextualize the concept of social identity in the
   Basque case.
3. Learn about the differences between objective and
   subjective vitality.
4. Examine the three vitality components of status,
   demographic factors, and institutional factors.

---

5. Evaluate the possible consequences of ethnolinguistic vitality.

REQUIRED READING

Giles, H., P. Garrett, and N. Coupland. 1988. "Language Acquisition in the Basque Country: Invoking and Extending the Intergroup Model," in *Conference on the Basque Language*, 299–310. Vitoria-Gasteiz: Basque Government Press.

Ros, M., C. Huici, and J. I. Cano. 1994. "Ethnolinguistic Vitality and Social Identity: Their Impact on Ingroup Bias and Social Attribution," *International Journal of the Sociology of Language*, vol. 108: 145–66.

SUGGESTED READING

Amorrortu, E. 2000a. *Linguistic Attitudes in the Basque Country: The Social Acceptance of a New Variety*, 164–72, 184–87. UMI: Univ. of Southern California.

Giles, H., R. Y. Bourhis, and Taylor. 1977. "Towards a Theory of Language in Ethnic Group Relations," in H. Giles (ed.), *Language, Ethnicity and Intergroup Relations*. New York: Academic Press.

WRITTEN LESSON FOR SUBMISSION

1. Taking everything you have learned so far into account, how important is the Basque language to Basque identity? Discuss this question in reference to Basque nationalism on one hand, and the American Basque community on the other.
2. Are there differences in the way Basques in Europe and those in America perceive their ethnicity, and in the role that language plays in both groups' identities?
3. Does the differing objective vitality of Basque in the European and American contexts influence the role

of language in their respective definitions of ethnicity?

4. Can we predict linguistic behavior (the use of a particular language or variety) from objective and/or subjective vitality data? How reliable is the vitality construct as a predictor of language use?

24 · Language and Ethnicity
Two Ethnic Communities

THIS CHAPTER examines the value of language in ethnicity perception in two different groups in the Basque Country. The two communities differ in the value that they give to Euskara in defining their ethnic identity. A highly Basque-speaking Gipuzkoan community assigns Euskara great importance as a marker of ethnicity (Urla, 1993b), whereas a highly Spanish-speaking community in borderland Araba rejects the association of Euskara with Basque identity (Hendry, 1997).

Ethnicity is an important factor in social categorization. According to social psychology literature, humans need to order their social environment by grouping people in a way that makes sense. Students of ethnicity focus on the boundaries that exist between groups. Boundary distinctiveness is the extent to which in-group and out-group members can easily be identified. Cultures with loose boundaries may change and converge, whereas cultures or ethnicities with clear boundaries will resist or diverge even more.

Ethnicity is an important factor in determining both self- and other-identity. Basque people are far from unanimous in their definitions of Basque ethnicity. Some stress that Basques share a set of values, history, culture, and language; others emphasize geography; and still others use even more subjective criteria, such as "the desire to be Basque" (Azurmendi, 1986: 383).

The Basque language itself defines a Basque person as someone who speaks Basque. *Euskalduna*, from *euskara + duna* (the Basque language + suffix that indicates possession) means etymologically 'Basque speaker', although many currently use it to refer to 'Basque person'.

One of the most important distinctions between Basque speakers and Spanish speakers is the differing value they assign to language as a characteristic of national and even ethnic identity. As Fishman (1991) points out, whereas for some people language may be an essential part of their ethnicity, others believe that they can be "as good a Xman without speaking Xish." This is a common attitude among Spanish-monolingual speakers. Of those interviewed in Bilbao—the biggest city of the Basque Country, in which a majority does not speak Basque—82% disagreed with the idea that it is impossible to be Basque without speaking the language, and only 12% agreed (Argüeso, 1988). In a study of youth attitudes, only 16% of those interviewed thought that "speaking Basque" was the main characteristic of Basque identity; for 73.4% of those interviewed, "the desire to be Basque" was the main attribute (Azurmendi, 1986: 383).

Urla (1993b) introduces us to a Basque nationalist community that assigns the Basque language a central place in its definition of Basque ethnicity. This community perceives the Basque language and culture (and, therefore, the *Basque essence*) to be at risk, and uses statistics to demonstrate this to the general public, raise consciousness among Basques, and generate support for RLS policy and planning. According to Urla, statistical practices shape the way Basques think and talk about themselves and challenge the linguistic status quo.

IN CONTRAST, Hendry (1997) reports feelings of inferiority among Rioja Arabans, who often feel that the Basque language should not be such a central ethnicity marker, and feel threatened by language planning efforts to reverse Euskara's minority status. Basque speakers usually assign strong integrative values to the Basque language, while Spanish speakers associate promotion of Basque with instrumental and political motivations on the part of its advocates.

THE IDENTIFICATION of language as a central feature of ethnicity is, of course, affected by political developments. A change can be observed since 1979, when, in a study conducted by Siadeco, 30.5% of Basque speakers and 28.2% of non-Basque speakers chose to define "the Basque language" as the most significant element of Basque identity (Azurmendi, 1998). Since the end of the Franco era, Basque has gained communicative functions as a result of the increase in its symbolic importance (Tejerina, 1992, 1996). However, the increase in communicative functions under democracy may have reduced the symbolic value of Basque. Since Basque is now an official language promoted by the Basque government, people who may have felt threatened during the Franco regime and the beginning of democracy may now feel more relaxed about the minority language.

More recent political developments and the polarization of political views into Basque nationalist and Spanish nationalist corners have led some to associate the Basque language with Basque nationalism. Social discourse about the *Basque language* reveals the differing influences of nationalist views (Jausoro, 1996). Basque nationalists use what Jausoro calls *affirmative discourse* and stress a necessary link between Euskara and the Basque Country. Groups that are not Basque nationalist produce a *discourse of indifference* and defend the view that Basque should be optional. Lastly, the *discourse of negation* ignores Basque because it is associated with the out-group (Basque speakers and nationalists).

The existence of groups opposing the promotion of the Basque language makes RLS policies and planning difficult. Obviously, the Basque language is not given the same degree of importance by Spanish monolin-

I'm a Basque!

People are not unanimous on their definition of ethnicity: for some speaking the language is at the essence, for others living in the country is enough, for others having Basque ancestors makes you Basque.

—————

guals that it is by bilinguals. In fact, we can speak of two ethnolinguistic communities in the BAC: a Spanish-monolingual community and a Basque- and Spanish-bilingual community.

—————

Lesson twenty-four

LEARNING OBJECTIVES

1. Compare the differing role that language plays in ethnic identity in Basque-speaking and non–Basque-speaking communities.

2. Pay attention to several types of discourse around the "Basque language" topic.

REQUIRED READING

Hendry, B. 1997. "Constructing Linguistic and Ethnic Boundaries in a Basque Borderland: Negotiating Identity in Rioja Alavesa, Spain." *Language Problems and Language Planning* 21(3): 216–33.

Urla, J. 1993b. "Cultural Politics in an Age of Statistics: Numbers, Nations, and the Making of Basque Identity," *American Ethnologist* 20(4): 818–43.

SUGGESTED READING

Argüeso, M. A. 1988. *Actualidad y perspectiva del euskera en Bilbao*. Austin: Univ. of Texas Press.

Azurmendi, M. J. 1986. "La juventud en Euskadi en relación al euskera," in *Juventud Vasca* 1986, 327–83, Vitoria-Gasteiz: Basque Government Press.

———. 1998. "Hizkuntza eta identitate etnosoziala Euskal Herrian," in M. J. Azurmendi (ed.), *Hizkuntza eta talde-nortasuna*, 237–65. Bilbao: Univ. of the Basque Country Press.

Fishman, J. 1991. *Reversing Language Shift*. Philadelphia: Multilingual Matters.

Jausoro, M. N. 1996. *La práctica discursiva y el interdiscurso: Una propuesta metodológica para la investigación social del euskera*. Leioa: Univ. of the Basque Country Press.

Tejerina, B. 1992. *Nacionalismo y lengua*. Madrid: Centro de Investigaciones Sociológicas.

———. 1996. "Language and Basque Nationalism: Collective Identity, Social Conflict and Institutionalisation," in C. Mar-Molinero and A. Smith (eds.), *Nationalism and the Nation in the Iberian Penin-*

sula: Competing and Conflicting Identities. Oxford: Berg.

Urla, J. 1987. *Being Basque, Speaking Basque.* UMI: Univ. of California-Berkeley.

WRITTEN LESSON FOR SUBMISSION

Federico Jiménez Losantos has said, "A foreigner could ask what the great hurry is, when eusquera has survived for two or three thousand years with little protection or none whatsoever. If eusquera is the minority language of the two spoken in the Basque Autonomous Community, if only about 15% of the population masters it, why should learning it, knowing it, and using it in public administration be mandatory? The imposition of the minority language, on the majority—even Basques of Basque origin—implies the prior delegitimization of the votes of 'outsiders,' which can in fact also be the votes of 'bad Basques'—in other words, non-nationalist" (1993, quoted in J. M. Torrealdai, 1998). Comment on this quotation from two different perspectives: (a) that of a Basque and Spanish bilingual, and (b) that of a Spanish-monolingual speaker. Take into account how a Basque nationalist and a Spanish nationalist might react to it.

25 · Rituals in favor of Euskara
Their connection to Basque ethnicity

THE GRASS-ROOTS revitalization movement often carries out rituals to support Basque. These rituals employ certain symbols as a clear way to define Basque ethnicity. This chapter addresses the manifestation of ethnic symbols in several of these popular rituals: Ikastola Days organized by the Confederation of Ikastolas and held in Iparralde (*Herri Urrats* 'Popular Step'), Navarre (*Nafarroa Oinez* 'Navarre on Foot'), Araba (*Araban Euskaraz* 'In Araba in Basque'), Biscay (*Ibilaldia* 'Stroll'), and Gipuzkoa (*Kilometroak* 'Kilometers'); AEK Eguna 'AEK Day' and ***Korrika*** 'Running', organized by AEK; the *Bateginik* 'All Together' campaign, organized by Euskal Kulturaren Batzarrea in 1988; and the *21. Mendeko Akordioa: Bai Euskarari* 'A 21st Century Agreement: Say Yes to Euskara' campaign, held in 1998 all over the Basque Country and organized by Kontseilua.

The rituals in support of the Basque language just listed share some common characteristics. First, they are organized by grass-root movements and held with a double objective in mind—not only to raise money for institutions that work for the normalization of Basque language use, but also to raise consciousness in Basque society on the precarious situation of Basque. Consciousness raising and fund-raising coexist in Basque-supporting events. Second, all the events are celebrated in a partylike and fun atmosphere. Despite the dangerous situation that is claimed for Euskara at all these events, the Basque language is associated with an optimistic and joyful attitude. Rituals in favor of Basque usually have music, dancing, games, and food, just like in any other good party. In addition, organizers project a dynamic image of Basque, adopting logos and slogans that stress movement and small but uninterrupted changes in the reversal language shift process, such as steps (Herri Urrats), strolls (Ibilaldia), running (Korrika), kilometers (Kilometroak), or movement on foot (Nafarroa Oinez).

Although there are always elements linked to Basque tradition, the association of Basque with modernity is increasingly emphasized. To give an example, we can comment on the motto of the latest AEK Eguna: *Metroz metro, beti euskaraz* 'Meter by meter, always in Basque'. This motto plays a word game, since *metro* also means 'subway' and makes a reference to the modern subway of Bilbao, where the AEK Eguna was held in 2002. Finally, rituals in favor of Euskara also share the display of nationalist Basque identity symbols, such as ikurrinas or Basque flags and different elements that stress territorial unity, such as maps or folklore manifestations representative of the whole Basque Country.

AMONG ALL the popular rituals in favor of Basque mentioned before, the one most studied is *Korrika* (Del Valle, 1994). *Korrika*, meaning 'running', is a fund-raising and consciousness-raising foot race organized by AEK. Thousands of runners of all ages from throughout the Basque Country run one-kilometer-long relays in a race that passes through the whole Basque Country over a nine-day period. A designated runner, most often representing a group that supports the Basque language, but sometimes a famous individual, carries the *testigo* 'baton/witness', which symbolizes the Basque language as a collective patrimony. Korrika, first held in 1980, continues as a biennial event.

Korrika stresses the active, militant character of Basque language promoters and the popular character of the language movement. In an attempt to link the past

Running for Basque
Korrika is a fund-raising and consciousness-raising foot race. It stresses the popular character of the language movement supporting Basque.

---

with the present, it combines traditional and modern references in a ritual full of ethnic symbols. In addition, this biennial event tries to resolve the following discontinuities and conflicts on a symbolic level (Del Valle, 1994: 1–37). On one hand, by running all over the Basque Country on both sides of the Pyrenees, organizers provide a symbolic contrast to the shrinking of geographical boundaries. The territories visited during the footrace are not only those in which Basque is still used, but also the ones in which Basque was once spoken but where family transmission has not continued.

On the other hand, a discontinuity in the generational transmission of Basque is resolved by the active presence of both older people and young children, who are often the carriers of the testigo, symbolizing the transmission of Basque. In addition, children can participate in their own *Korrika Txikia* 'Small Korrika'.

FINALLY, the contradiction between the responsibility socially assigned to women in the transmission of the language and the minor role held by women in the organization of the first Korrikas was resolved in subsequent events after the right of women to participate directly was demanded and achieved.

Lesson twenty-five

LEARNING OBJECTIVES
1. Identify popular cultural markers in the Basque language revitalization movement.
2. Examine how discontinuities and conflicts related to the Basque language are resolved in Korrika, a ritual in support of Basque.
3. Situate the Korrika in the context of social movements supporting Basque.
4. Explore the display of ethnic symbols in Korrika and other popular rituals in favor of Basque.

REQUIRED READING
Del Valle, T. 1994. *Korrika: Basque Ritual for Ethnic Identity*, i–xi, 1–37. Reno: Univ. of Nevada Press.

SUGGESTED READING
Del Valle, T. 1994. *Korrika: Basque Ritual for Ethnic Identity*. Reno: Univ. of Nevada Press (the rest of the book).
Multiple authors. 1999a. *Euskararen aldeko gizarte-mogimendua eta EKB, azken 25 urteak gainbegi-*

ratuz, monographic number of *Bat Soziolinguistika Aldizkaria,* no. 31.

Multiple authors 1999b. *Kontseilua,* monographic number of *Jakin,* no. 112.

INTERNET RESOURCES

Korrika homepage (only available in Basque): http://www.korrika.org

The website of the Confederation of Ikastolas contains the logos of all the Ikastola Days held in Herri Urrats, Nafarroa Oinez, Ibilaldia, Kilometroak, and Araban Euskaraz: http://www.ikastola.net

The main objective of Kontseilua (the Board of Basque Language Corporate Institutions) is "the normalization of the Basque language by means of a major consensus which provides for a strategic plan to ensure complete development of the language and strengthening of relations among the different sectors of Basque cultural activity." Kontseilua's website contains a great deal of information in English: http://www.kontseilua.org

WRITTEN LESSON FOR SUBMISSION

1. Explain two ethnic symbols used in Korrika.
2. What does the testigo symbolize in Korrika?
3. In your opinion, what is the importance of popular events in favor of the Basque language for reversing language shift?
4. Are popular rituals in favor of Euskara important for a definition of Basque identity? How so?

26 · Language and Alternative Culture

POPULAR cultural displays demonstrate language ideology among popular and alternative social groups. Very often, scholars focus on "official" or mainstream language ideology. In the process, they ignore alternative displays that may be equally, or even more, influential in language use among young speakers. This chapter examines some popular cultural displays among youths engaged in the Basque revival movement.

In contrast to the "official" reversing language shift planning and standardization movement, which stressed the legalization of Basque and "correct" Basque language use, popular culture makes use of outlaw publicity and parody and language internal variation as a way of expressing criticism of Spanish linguistic domination.

As Urla (1995) points out, "in the years since Franco's death, one finds among Basque radical nationalist youth a self conscious attempt to make use of intentionally marginal or 'outlaw' publicity—street graffiti, zines, low-power free radio—as well as a lively rock music scene, to give voice to their minoritized language and their not-so-polite critiques of the state, consumer capitalism, police repression, and a host of other social concerns."

Distancing themselves from the dominant public discourse of the officialist "modern" or "rational" language movement, Basque radical nationalist youth intentionally uses marginal (outlaw) publicity and linguistic practices to give voice to Euskara and offer a political critic of Basque society. For instance, Urla (1995) points to the use of hika on free radio to address those occupying higher social status as a way of rejecting traditional status hierarchies. Although Basque sociolinguistic rules do not allow for the use of hika to a person holding

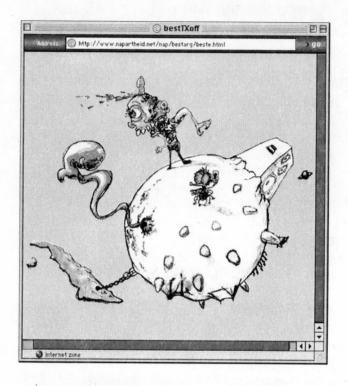

Supporting Basque from alternative culture
Distancing themselves from the officialist language
movement, Napartheid fanzine cartoonists offer a political critic of Basque society while supporting the language.
Screen shot from the <www.napartheid.net> website.

higher status, youths may use this form intentionally.
By breaking sociolinguistic rules, youths contest mainstream linguistic and social practices.

Free-radio broadcasters and magazine creators often
also use register and dialectal variation for expressive
purposes, again distancing themselves from prescrip-

tivists. In a fanzine called *Napartheid*, for example, cartoonists criticize the marginalization and folkloric treatment of Euskara pervasive in the mass media by inserting traditional Basque elements as illustrations accompanied by a Spanish text written with Basque spelling and incorrect grammar (see Urla, 1999, example 1). As Urla also points out, "while a good part of the Basque-language revival has worked compensatorily to improve the status of Basque by modeling good, proper, or literate Euskara, this lowbrow humor embraces precisely stigmatized qualities of anarchic variability and illiteracy as a means of rejecting Spanish domination."

The dominance of English, as the language of globalization, and its intrusion in the dialect of the youth, since it is often considered cool and innovative, are also criticized. In Urla's (1999) Figure 2, a Cro-Magnon-looking guy serves as a guardian of Basque language and culture, in contrast to a silly-looking, Americanized guy in expensive American-brand clothes. The former claims the use of Basque by parodying the use of English words among young Basques, by adding a letter G to the word *hitzegin* 'speak' to make it look like frequently used hybrids such as trekking, puenting, or zapping.

ANOTHER way of contesting linguistic domination is through the parody of symbolic uses of Basque: non-Basque speakers often code switch to a few Basque lexical items when speaking in Spanish to demonstrate their Basque nationalist pedigree.

In sum, through the use of parody, humor, and internally and externally induced variation, Basque youth also contribute to reversing language shift in their own way, while differing from the rational, "standardizing," official revitalization movement.

Lesson twenty-six

LEARNING OBJECTIVES
1. Consider "alternative" versus "rational" reversal language shift efforts.
2. Examine parody and humor as strategies to criticize language-related issues.

REQUIRED READING

Urla, J. 1995. "Outlaw Language: Creating Alternative Public Spheres in Basque Free Radio," *Pragmatics* 5(2): 245–61.

Urla, J. 1999. "Basque Language Revival and Popular Culture," in W. A. Douglass et al. (eds.), *Basque Cultural Studies*, 44–62. Reno: Basque Studies Program.

INTERNET RESOURCES

Website of a fanzine created in 1988 with the objective of criticizing the Law of Officialization of Basque in Navarre. The name of the fanzine, Napartheid, makes reference to the discrimination Navarrese Basque speakers suffer: The Law discriminates against Basque speakers just as apartheid discriminated against blacks. You can see all the issues published to date online (in Basque only): http://www.napartheid.net

WRITTEN LESSON FOR SUBMISSION
1. Comment on the differences and similarities between the "official" standardization movement and the popular "alternative" movement.
2. Urla states that "we will want to look at forms of popular culture not to measure their 'contamination' by other cultures and languages, but as expressive of newly forged social experiences and identities. The

point is not to evaluate what is being 'lost' or 'retained' in Basque culture, but what Basque culture and identity is coming to mean to young people" (1999: 59). Critically evaluate Urla's statement. Take all that you have learned through working with this book into consideration: linguistic and cultural permeability (linguistic change, language-contact, linguistic purism), definitions of Basque identity, and the "official" and popular reversing language shift movements.

Glossary

Affricate: Sound produced with a complete closure of the oral tract, then a release (as when a stop is produced), and a continuation (as in a fricative).

Agglutinative language: A morphological characteristic. Words can be divided in distinct prefixes and suffixes.

Autonomous community: Administrative and political entity within the Spanish State. Similar to states in the United States of America.

Borrowing: A word incorporated into the system from another language. Also called a *loanword*.

Codification: A type of language planning. Creation of new forms or agreement on which regional, social, or situational variant should be favored.

Communicative competence: The ability not only to know linguistic features, but also to know how to use them appropriately.

Compounding: To put words together to create new concepts. For example: *aurreritzi* (aurre + iritzi) 'prejudice' (lit. before + opinion); *eragozpide* (eragotzi + bide) 'obstacle' (lit. to object + way); *etxejabe* (etxe + jabe) 'homeowner' (lit. home + owner).

Consonants: Sounds produced by partially or completely blocking air when it goes from the lungs through the vocal tract.

Discourse marker: Sequentially dependent elements which bracket units of talk and provide local and global coherence. For instance, English *well, ok, so, you know*.

Ergative language: A language that does not mark differently the subject of an intransitive verb and the direct object of a transitive verb, but marks differently the subject of a transitive and an intransitive verb.

Flap rhotic: Sound produced by the tongue tip hitting the alveolar ridge at a high speed.

Fricative: When a fricative sound is produced, air passes continuously through a narrow opening.

Gaueskolas: 'Night schools'; schools created in the 1960s in the Basque Country to teach Basque to adults.

Grammatical gender: In some languages, nouns can have grammatical gender, which is opposed to natural gender. The latter is given by the semantics of the noun and it is logical: Male beings are masculine, female beings are feminine, and no living entities are neuter. In languages with grammatical gender, the meaning of the noun does not count for gender assignment. Each noun needs to be memorized with its gender. Old English, German, French, and Spanish are examples of languages that have grammatical gender.

Head-final: Structural characteristic of certain languages by which modifiers precede their head, for instance Basque *etorri den mutila* (come AUX: rel boy: abs) 'the boy who came'.

Ikastolas: Basque primary schools in which the language of instruction is Basque. There was a big grass-root movement of ikastolas in the 1960s.

Isolate: A language that cannot be related genetically to any other language known; for instance, Basque.

Korrika: 'Running'; a fund-raising event organized every two years by AEK in support of Basque.

Linguistic models: Basque educational models. They are based on the language of instruction used. Model A and D use Spanish and Basque, respectively, as the medium of instruction, whereas Model B uses both languages.

Literary dialects: Regional dialects that have traditionally been used in written and have undergone a certain process of standardization.

Morpheme: A meaningful linguistic unit that cannot be divided into smaller meaningful parts.

Nasal: A sound produced when air goes through the nasal cavity instead of through the oral cavity.

National language: The most used language in a community.

Neologism: A recently made-up word.

Official language: The language promoted by law.

Palatal: A sound produced by touching the palate or velum with the tongue.

Permeability: Characteristic of a language; capacity to adopt features from an external system.

Prescriptivism: Establishing correct usage, specifying what should be used and what should not.

Public institutions: Governmental institutions: the Basque government, provincial governments, and city councils. In the Basque context, public institutions are also referred to as "the public administration."

Purism: Related to prescriptivism. Promoting "pure" linguistic forms or forms that have not received the external influence of another language.

Sibilant: Sounds marked by a high-pitched hissing sound quality.

Stop: A sound produced when air is built up in the vocal tract and suddenly released through the mouth.

Stress: Related to loudness. Variations in loudness express the difference between stressed and unstressed syllables. Different stress patterns may indicate differences in meaning.

Tone: Related to pitch. Variations in pitch distinguish different words.

Transfer: Adoption by a language of a linguistic feature borrowed from another language.

Trill rhotic: A sound produced with vibration of the tip of the tongue as in the Spanish word *perro*.

Variant: A form out of a set of forms. For example, two spellings of the same word or two lexical items with the same meaning used in different dialects would be variants.

Variety: A language, dialect, or register.

Velar: A consonant produced by the tongue approaching or touching the roof of the mouth at the velum.

Voiced sounds: Sounds produced with closed and vibrating vocal cords.

Vowels: Sounds produced with no blocking of air.

List of Abbreviations

LINGUISTIC

Abl	ablative case
Abs	absolutive case
Asp	aspect
AUX	auxiliary verb
Dat	dative case
DO	direct object
Erg	ergative case
F	female addressee
H	high
Ind	indicative
Ines	inessive case
IO	indirect object
L	low
M	male addressee
O	object
Obj	object
Pl	plural
Poss	possessive case
Pot	potential
Pres	present tense
S	subject
Sg	singular
T	*tu* (or familiar)
V	verb
V	*vos* (or formal)

GENERAL

AB	American Basque
AED	*Arrasate Euskaldun Dezagun* 'Let's Basquisize Arrasate'

AEK	*Alfabetatze eta Euskalduntze Koordinakundea* 'Association of Basquization and Literarization'
ANOVA	analysis of variance
BAC	Basque Autonomous Community
EB	Emigré Basque
EHE	*Euskal Herrian Euskaraz* 'The Basque Country in Basque'
EITB	Basque Radio and Television
EKB	*Euskal Kultur Batzarrea* 'The Congress of Basque Culture'
ELV	ethnolinguistic vitality theory
ETA	*Euzkadi Ta Askatasuna* 'Basque Homeland and Liberty'
FB	Full Basque
HABE	Institute for Adult Literacy and Basquization
IK	*Ikastolen Konfederakundea* 'Association of Ikastolas'
IPA	International Phonetic Alphabet
LSA	Language Society of America
MG	matched guise
PCA	Principal Components Analysis
RB	Reduced Basque
RLS	reversing language shift
SD	semantic differential
UEU	*Udako Euskal Unibertsitatea* 'Basque Summer University'
UZEI	Basque Center for Terminology and Lexicography

Works Cited

Alberdi, J. 1995. "The Development of the Basque System of Terms of Address and the Allocutive Conjugation," in J. I. Hualde, J. A. Lakarra, and R. L. Trask (eds.), *Towards a History of the Basque Language*. Amsterdam/Philadephia: John Benjamins Publ.

———. 1996. *Euskararen tratamenduak, erabilera*. Bilbao: Royal Academy of the Basque Language.

Altuna, O. 1998. "Euskararen kale erabilpena Euskal Herrian," *Bat Soziolinguistika Aldizkaria*, no. 28: 15–64.

Amorrortu, E. 1995. "Retention and Accommodation in the Basque of Elko, Nevada," in *Anuario de Filología Vasca Julio de Urquijo*, vol. 29, no. 2, 407–29. Donostia: Gipuzkoako Foru Aldundia.

———. 2000a. *Linguistic Attitudes in the Basque Country: The Social Acceptance of a New Variety*. UMI: Univ. of Southern California.

———. 2000b. "Is American Basque a Unified Variety? Structural Changes in the Basque of Elko, Nevada," *Journal of Basque Studies*, vol. 20, 105–18.

———. 2001a. "Métodos indirectos en la medición de actitudes lingüísticas: El euskara frente al castellano," in A. I. Moreno (ed.), *Perspectivas Recientes sobre el Discurso/Recent Perspectives on Discourse*. León: Servicio de Publicaciones de la Universidad de León y Aesla.

———. 2001b. "Unibertsitate-ikasleen euskalki eta batuarekiko jarrerak," in *Mendebalde Euskal Kultur Alkartea, Euskalkia eta Hezkuntza*, 61–80. Bilbao: Mendebalde Euskal Kultur Alkartea.

———. 2001c. "The Discourse and Social Use of DM Bueno in Eight- and Ten-Year Old Basque-Speaking

Children," in *Research on Child Language Acquisition*. Proceedings of the8th Conference of the International Association for the Study of Child Language, Almgren, M.; Barreña, A.; Ezeizabarrena, M. J.; MacWhinney, B. (eds.), 250–63. Somerville, MA: Cascadilla Press.

Argüeso, M. A. 1988. *Actualidad y perspectiva del euskera en Bilbao*. Austin: Univ. of Texas Press.

Aske, J. 1997. *Basque Word Order and Disorder: Principles, Variation, and Prospects*. Ph.D dissertation. UMI: Univ. of California, Berkeley.

Aulestia, Gorka. 1995. *Improvisational Poetry from the Basque Country*. Reno: Univ. of Nevada Press.

Azurmendi, M. J. 1983. "Algunos aspectos del Euskara utilizados hoy," *Iker* 2: 175–87.

———. 1986. "La juventud en Euskadi en relación al euskera," in *Juventud Vasca 1986*, 327–83, Vitoria-Gasteiz: Basque Government Press.

———. 1998. "Hizkuntza eta identitate etnosoziala Euskal Herrian," in M. J. Azurmendi (ed.), *Hizkuntza eta talde-nortasuna*, 237–65. Bilbao: Univ. of the Basque Country Press.

Bakker, P. 1989. " 'The Language of the Coast Tribes Is Half Basque': A Basque-American Indian Pidgin, 1540–1640," *Anthropological Linguistics* 31(3–4): 117–48.

Basque Government. 1996. *Sociolinguistic Study of the Basque Country 1996: The Continuity of Basque 2*. Vitoria-Gasteiz: Basque Government Press.

———. 1998. *General Plan for Promoting Basque Language Use*. Vitoria-Gasteiz: Basque Government.

———. 2000. Report on the Language Policy in the Basque Autonomous Community.

Brown, R., and A. Gilman. 1960. "The Pronouns of Power and Solidarity," in T. A. Sebeok (ed.), *Style in*

Language, 253–76. New York: Technology Press of MIT.

Del Valle, T. 1994. *Korrika: Basque Ritual for Ethnic Identity*. Reno: Univ. of Nevada Press.

De Rijk, R. P. 1998. "Familiarity or Solidarity: The Pronoun Hi in Basque," in *De Lingua Vasconum*, 297–300. Supplements of the *Anuario del Seminario de Filología Vasca Julio de Urquijo*. Bilbao: Univ. of the Basque Country.

Douglass, W. A., and J. Bilbao. 1975. "Ethnicity Maintenance among Basque-Americans," in *Amerikanuak: Basques in the New World*. Reno: Univ. of Nevada Press.

Echano, A. 1989. *Attitudes toward Euskera: Using the Matched-Guise Technique among School Children in the Basque Country*. Unpublished dissertation, Univ. of Edinburgh.

Echeverria, B. 2000. *The Gendering of Basque Ethnic Identity*. UMI: Univ. of California, San Diego.

Edwards, J., and H. Giles. 1984. "Applications of the Social Psychology of Language: Sociolinguistics and Education," in P. Trudgill (ed.), *Applied Sociolinguistics*. London: Academic Press.

Elordui, A. 1999. "Processes of Language Shift and Loss: Evidence from Basque," in *Studies in Multilingualism*. Tilburg: Univ. Press.

Elosua, P.; López, A.; and Artamendi, J. A. 1994. "Elebitasunari buruzko testaren bidez lorturiko datuen azterketa kuantitatiboa," *Tantak* 12: 197–217.

Erize, X. 1997. *Nafarroako Euskararen Historia Soziolinguistikoa 1863–1936*. Iruña: Navarrese Government Press.

Etxeberria, F. 1987. *El fracaso de la escuela*. San Sebastián: Erein.

Etxeberria, F. 1999. *Bilingüismo y Educación en el País del Euskara*. Donostia: Erein.

Etxeberria, F. and Aierbe, P. 1988. "Eskolako Euskal Elebitasunaren Ikerketa," *II Euskal Mundu Biltzarra. Euskara Biltzarra*, vol. 2: 130–35.

Euskaltzaindia. 1998. Euskara Batuaren Ahoskera Landua. Approved on Oct. 9, 1998: http://www.euskaltzaindia.net

Ferguson, Ch. 1959. "Diglossia," *Word* 15: 325–40.

Fernández de Larrinoa, K. 1992. *Estatu Batuetako mendebalde urrutiko euskal jaiak*. Vitoria-Gasteiz: Basque Government Press.

Finegan, E. (n.d.) "What Is 'Correct' Language?" Language Society of America webpage: http://www.lsadc.org/Finegan.html

Finegan, E., and D. Biber. 1994. "Register and Social Dialect Variation: An Integrated Approach," in D. Biber and E. Finegan (eds.), *Sociolinguistic Perspectives on Register*. New York: Oxford Univ. Press.

Fishman, J. A. 1991. *Reversing Language Shift: Theoretical and Empirical Foundations of Assistance to Threatened Languages*. Philadelphia: Multilingual Matters.

Gaminde, I. 1998. *Euskaldunen azentuak*. Bilbao: Labayru Ikastegia.

Garaialde, I., et al. 1998. "Modeling the Long Term Future of the Basque Language," 1–15. Paper presented at the *Basques in the Contemporary World: Migration, Identity, and Globalization* Conference, Reno.

Gardner, R. C. and Lambert, W. E. 1972. *Attitudes and Motivations in Second-Language Learning*. Rowley, Mass.: Newbury House Publ.

Giles, H., R. Y. Bourhis, and Taylor. 1977. "Towards a Theory of Language in Ethnic Group Relations," in

H. Giles (ed.), *Language, Ethnicity and Intergroup Relations*. New York: Academic Press.

Giles, H., P. Garrett, and N. Coupland. 1988. "Language Acquisition in the Basque Country: Invoking and Extending the Intergroup Model," in *Conference on the Basque Language*, 299–310. Vitoria-Gasteiz: Basque Government Press.

Haugen, E. 1997 [1966]. "Language Standardization," in N. Coupland and A. Jaworsky (eds.), *Sociolinguistics: A Reader and Coursebook*, 341–52. Hampshire and London: MacMillan Press Ltd.

Hendry, B. 1997. "Constructing Linguistic and Ethnic Boundaries in a Basque Borderland: Negotiating Identity in Rioja Alavesa, Spain," *Language Problems and Language Planning* 21(3): 216–33.

Hualde, J. I. 1988. "Euskararen ume ezezaguna: Euskal Herriko bale arrantzaleen truke-hizkuntza," *Jakin*, vol. 48: 53–62.

———. 1991a. *Basque Phonology*. London: Routledge.

———. 1991b. "Icelandic Basque Pidgin," *Anuario del Seminario de Filología Vasca Julio de Urquijo* 25(2): 427–37.

Hualde, J. I., G. Elordieta, and A. Elordieta. 1994. *The Basque dialect of Lekeitio*, supplements of *Anuario del Seminario de Filología Julio de Urquijo*, no. 34. Bilbao and San Sebastian: Univ. of the Basque Country and Diputación Foral de Gipuzkoa.

Hymes, D. 1972. "On Communicative Competence," in J. B. Pride and J. Holmes (eds.), *Sociolinguistics: Selected Readings*, Baltimore: Penguin.

Intxausti, J. 1995. *Euskal Herria the Country of the Basque Language*. Vitoria-Gasteiz: the Basque Government Press.

Jacobsen, W. H. 1999. "Basque Language Origin Theories," in W. A. Douglass et al. (eds.), *Basque Cultural Studies*, 27–43. Reno: Basque Studies Program.

Jausoro, M. N. 1996. *La práctica discursiva y el interdiscurso: Una propuesta metodológica para la investigación social del euskera*. Leioa: Univ. of the Basque Country Press.

Kurlansky, M. 1999. *The Basque History of the World*. London: Jonathan Cape.

Lafitte, P. 1979 [1962] *Grammaire basque (Navarro-Labourdin littéraire)*. Donostia: Elkar.

Landa, A., and A. Elordui. 2000. "Sobre las gramáticas bilingües y la permeabilidad estructural," in *Estudios de Lingüística Inglesa Aplicada*.

Larrañaga, I. 1998. "Euskararen Egoerari Buruzko Ikerketak: Euforia-Giroa eta Konfusio-Zeremonia," *Zenbat Gara Bizitza eta Hizkuntza Aldizkaria*, no. 3: 18–31.

Lekuona, Juan Mari. 1982. *Ahozko Euskal Literatura*. Donostia: Erein.

MacClancy, J. 1996. "Bilingualism and Multinationalism in the Basque Country," in C. Mar-Molinero and A. Smith (eds.), *Nationalism and the Nation in the Iberian Peninsula: Competing and Conflicting Identities*, pp. 207–20. Berg: Oxford.

Multiple authors. 1999a. *Euskararen aldeko gizarte-mogimendua eta EKB, azken 25 urteak gainbegiratuz*, monographic number of *Bat Soziolinguistika Aldizkaria*, no. 31.

Multiple authors. 1999b. *Kontseilua*, monographic number of *Jakin*, no. 112.

Martínez-Arbelaiz, A. 1996. "The Language Requirement Outside the Academic Setting: The Case of the Basque Administration," *Journal of Multilingual and Multicultural Development* 17(5): 359–72.

Milroy, L., and D. Preston. 1999. "Introduction," *Journal of Language and Social Psychology* 18(1): 4–9.

Mitxelena, K. 1988. "Relaciones de parentesco de la lengua vasca," in *Sobre Historia de la Lengua Vasca, Supplements of the Anuario del Seminario de Filología Vasca "Julio de Urquijo"* 10, 56–73.

Rodríguez, F. 1993. "Unity of the Basque Language and Basque Political Unity," originally published in *Basque in Uztaro* 9, translated by Alan King: http://ibs.lgu.ac.uk/forum/Iborn.htm

Romaine, S. 1996. "Bilingualism," in W. C. Ritchie and T. K. Bhatia (eds.), *Handbook of Second Language Acquisition*, 57 1–604. San Diego: Academic Press.

Ros, M., C. Huici, and J. I. Cano. 1994. "Ethnolinguistic Vitality and Social Identity: Their Impact on Ingroup Bias and Social Attribution," *International Journal of the Sociology of Language*, vol. 108: 145–66.

Sánchez Carrión, J. M. 1991. *Un futuro para nuestro pasado. Claves para la recuperación del Euskara y teoría social de las lenguas.* San Sebastian: Seminario de Filología Vasca Julio de Urquijo and Adorez eta Atseginez Mintegia.

Segura, S., and Etxebarria, J. M. 1996. *Del Latín al Euskara: Latinetik Euskarara.* Bilbao: Univ. of Deusto.

Silva-Corvalán, C. 1994. *Language Contact and Change: Spanish in Los Angeles.* Oxford: Clarendon Press.

Tejerina, B. 1992. *Nacionalismo y Lengua.* Madrid: Siglo XXI.

———. 1996. "Language and Basque Nationalism: Collective Identity, Social Conflict and Institutionalisation," in Mar-Molinero and Smith (eds.), *Nationalism and the Nation in the Iberian Peninsula.* Competing and Conflicting Identities, 221–36. Berg: Oxford.

Thomason, S. G., and T. Kaufman. 1988. *Language Contact, Creolization, and Genetic Linguistics*. Berkeley: Univ. of California Press.

Torrealdai, J. M. 1998. *El Libro Negro del Euskera*. Donostia: Ttarttalo.

Trask, R. L. 1997. *The History of Basque*. London and New York: Routledge.

———. (n.d.a) "A Linguistic Sketch of Basque": http://www.cogs.susx.ac.uk/users/larryt/basque.sketch.html

———. (n.d.b) "FAQs about Basque and the Basques," pp. 1–6: http://www.cogs.susx.ac.uk/users/larryt/basque.faqs.html

———. (n.d.c) "Some Important Basque Words (And a Bit of Culture)," pp. 1–17: http://www.cogs.susx.ac.uk/users/larryt/basque.words.html

———. (n.d.d) "Prehistory and Connections with Other Languages": http://www.cogs.susx.ac.uk/users/larry/basque.prehistory.html

Trudgill, P. 1974. *The Social Differentiation of English in Norwich*. Cambridge: Cambridge Univ. Press.

Txillardegi et al. 1987. *Dialektologiaren Hastapenak*. Iruiñea: Udako Euskal Unibertsitatea.

Urla, J. 1987. *Being Basque, Speaking Basque*. UMI: Univ. of California, Berkeley.

———. 1993a) "Contesting Modernities: Language Standardization and the Making of an Ancient/Modern Basque Culture," *Critique of Anthropology* 13(2): 101–18.

———. 1993b. "Cultural Politics in an Age of Statistics: Numbers, Nations, and the Making of Basque Identity," *American Ethnologist* 20(4): 818–843.

———. 1995. "Outlaw Language: Creating Alternative Public Spheres in Basque Free Radio," *Pragmatics* 5(2): 245–61.

Urla, J. 1999. "Basque Language Revival and Popular Culture," in W. A. Douglass et al. (eds.), *Basque Cultural Studies*, 44–62. Reno: Basque Studies Program.

Weinrich, U. 1974. *Languages in Contact.* The Hague: Mouton.

Yrizar, Pedro. 1981. *Contribución a la dialectología de la lengua vasca.* Donostia: Caja de Ahorros Provincial.

Zuazo, K. 1988. *Euskararen Batasuna.* Bilbao: Royal Academy of the Basque Language.

———. 1995. "The Basque Country and the Basque Language: An Overview of the External History of the Basque Language," in J. I. Hualde, J. A. Lakarra, and R. L. Trask (eds.), *Towards a History of the Basque Language,* 5–30. Amsterdam/Philadelphia: John Benjamins Publ.

———. 1998. "Euskalkiak, gaur," *Fontes Linguae Vasconum* 78: 191–233.

Zulaika, J. 1988. "The Bertsolariak," in *Basque violence: Metaphor and Sacrament,* 209–30. Reno: Univ. of Nevada Press.

Internet Sites

AEK homepage
Aholab
Argia
Association of Ikastolas
Aurki information search engine
Basque Government site, Department of Culture
Basque Institute of Statistics
Basque Radio and Television (EITB)
Berria, former Euskaldunon Egunkaria
Bertsolari magazine
Bizkaieraren fonotekea
Blas Uberuaga's Basque page
Department of Education, Universities and Research of
    the Basque Government
Deputy Ministry for Language Policy of the Basque Gov-
    ernment
Estornés Lasa's Basque Encyclopedia
Euskal Herrian Euskaraz
Euskalterm database
Euskaltzaindia
Euskararen Kontseilua
Eusko Ikaskuntza homepage
HABE
Jalgi information search engine
Kaixo information search engine
Korrika
Labayru Ikastegia
Language Society of America (LSA)
Larry Trask's Page
Mendebalde Kultur Alkartea homepage
Morris English-Basque online dictionary
Napartheid fanzine

Udako Euskal Unibertsitatea (UEU)
UZEI

Pictures

Index

A

AB, American Basque, 194

Abl, ablative case, 194

Abs, absolutive case, 194

Academy of the Basque Language, created in 1918 to regulate spelling, to codify new lexicon and to enhance literary Basque, 57

Acceleration, linguistic phenomena. Began in Europe and accelerated in the diaspora, 134

Accommodation phenomena, brought about the creation of inter-dialectal forms present in neither dialect, 133

Acquisition planning, organized efforts to promote the learning of a language, 42

Act of Normalization of the Basque Language establishes Advisory Board, 43

guarantee co-official status to Basque, 43

regulation of linguistic models and Institute for Adult Literacy and Basquization, 43

AED (*Arrasate Euskaldun Dezagun* 'Let's Basquisize Arrasate'), 45, 194

AEK (*Alfabetatze eta Euskalduntze Koordinakundea*) 'Association of Basquization and Literarization', 195

'Day', 180

dedicated to Basque L2 teaching, 161

homepage, 54, 205

teach Basque to adults, 53

affirmative discourse, stress a necessary link between Euskara and the Basque Country, 176

affricate, sound produced with a complete closure of oral tract, then a release and a continuation, 190

agglutinative language, 32

words can be divided in distinct prefixes and suffixes, 190

Aholab, 39, 205

Alberdi (1995 & 1996), 147, 148, 150, 152, 156, 196

hika ...
  women generally use less than men because show greater
    concern for politeness and social relations, 154
Hualde, J. I., J. A. Lakarra, and R. L. Trask (1995), 25
Hualde, J. I., (1988), 124
Hualde, J. I., (1991a), 38
Hualde, J. I., (1991b), 123
Hualde, J. I., G. Elordieta, and A. Elordieta. (1994), 38
Huescan market
  use of Basque along with Hebrew and Arabic prohibited in
    fourteenth-century, 19

I

Iberian, 28
Icelandic Basque, interaction between Basque fishermen and
  Icelandic natives, 121
IK, *Ikastolen Konfederakundea* 'Association of Ikastolas', 195
Ikastola days, 180
Ikastolas, 161
  and gaueskolas, creation of, 24
  Basque primary schools in which the language of instruc-
    tion is Basque, 191
  developed the Model D (full immersion in Basque) of pri-
    mary education system, 49
  primary and/or secondary education schools where Basque
    is medium of communication and instruction, 43
Ikastolen Konfederakundea (IK), engaged in primary and secondary education, 53
incongruity between language knowledge and use: interaction
  difficult, minority status and previous stigmatization, only
  master formal register of Basque, 69
Ind, indicative, 194
individual bilingualism, ability of a person to speak two languages, 116
Ines, inessive case, 194
in-group bias of Basque speakers toward the minority language, 169

Krutwig

    intellectual articulation of the role that language plays in national identity, 159

    political reasons for establishing a unified variety as correct usage, culture language, national language, 58

Kurlansky (1999), 17

L

L, low variety, 194

Labayru Ikastegia, 52, 53, 54, 199, 205

    homepage, 54

    institute, Basque language and literature classes to Biscayan adult native speakers since 1970, 52

    teach Basque to adults, 53

Labourdin

    almost only dialect used in written literature until eighteenth century, 97

    literary dialect, school of Sare and its leader Axular, contributed to creation of, 20

lack of preference toward Basque speakers along solidarity dimension, points to need to stress integrative motivations for learning and using minority language, 77

Lafitte, P. (1979 [1962]), 39

Landa, A., and A. Elordui (2000), 113

Language, Society and Culture: main objectives of Basque Sociolinguistics, 7

language

    as characteristic of national and ethnic identity, important distinctions between Basque speakers and Spanish speakers is differing value they assign to, 175

    competence in BAC, 65

    disappears, because those who know it do not use it, 108

    shift, 41

    universals, basic principles that govern structure of all or most languages, 29

Language Society of America, 195, 205

Lapurtera Klasikoa. See Literary Labourdin

Colophon

This book was edited by Nancy G. Carleton and indexed by Lawrence Feldman. It was laid out and produced by Gunnlaugur SE Briem, who also designed the typeface, BriemAnvil.

It was printed and bound by Fidlar Doubleday of Kalamazoo, Michigan.

The Basque Studies textbook series

1. Basque Cinema: An Introduction
2. Basque Culture: Anthropological Perspectives
3. Basque Cyberculture: From Digital Euskadi to CyberEuskalherria
4. Basque Diaspora; Migration and Transnational Identity
5. Basque Economy: From Industrialization to Globalization
6. Basque Gender Studies
7. Basque Sociolinguistics; Language, Society, and Culture
8. Basque Sociology; Society, Identity, and Politics
9. Guggenheim Bilbao Museoa: Museums, Architecture, and City Renewal
10. Modern Basque History: Eighteenth Century to the Present
11. Waking the Hedgehog; The Literary Universe of Bernardo Atxaga